POPE PIUS XII LIBRARY, ST. JOSEPH COL.

3 2528 07056 3228

The Writings of Margaret of Oingt
Medieval Prioress and Mystic

D1528023

The Focus Library of Medieval Women
Series Editor • Jane Chance

Christine de Pizan's Letter of Othea to Hector • Jane Chance • 1990
Margaret of Oingt, Medieval Prioress and Mystic • Renate Blumenfeld-Kosinski • 1990

Forthcoming

St. Bridget of Sweden Writings • Julia Bolton Holloway • 1990
Cloistered Women: 14th Century German Convent Literature • Rosemary Hale • 1991
Hrotsvit of Gandersheim Lengends • Katharina Wilson • 1992

The Focus Classical Library
Series Editors • James J. Clauss and Michael Halleran

Hesiod's Theogony • Richard Caldwell • 1987
The Heracles of Euripides • Michael Halleran • 1988
Aristophanes' Lysistrata • Jeffrey Henderson • 1988

Forthcoming

Oedipus at Colonus • Mary Whitlock Blundell • 1990
Medea • A. J. Podlecki • 1989
Lucretius On The Nature of Things • Walter Englert • 1990
The Argonautica • James J. Clauss • 1991
The Trachae • Richard Martin • 1991

The Writings of Margaret of Oingt Medieval Prioress and Mystic
(D. 1310)

Translated from the Latin and Francoprovençal
With an Introduction, Essay and Notes

Renate Blumenfeld-Kosinski
Columbia University

Copyright © 1990 Renate Blumenfeld-Kosinski
Printed in the United States of America

Reissued 1997
D.S. Brewer, Cambridge

ISBN 0 85991 442 9

D.S. Brewer is an imprint of
Boydell & Brewer Ltd
PO Box 9, Woodbridge, Suffolk IP12 3DF
and Boydell & Brewer Inc.
PO Box 41026, Rochester, NY 14604-4126, USA

Cover: Anonymous, South German, late 15th-early 16th century, Four female saints (St. Agatha, St. Dorothea, St. Barbara, and unidentified martyr saint), tempera on wooden panel. Reproduced with permission of The Art Museum, Princeton University. Museum purchase, John Maclean Magie and Gertrude Magie Fund.

The text has been printed on recycled paper.

This book is published by Focus Information Group, Inc., PO Box 369, Newburyport, MA 01950. All rights reserved. No part of this publication may be reproduced, stored in a retrieval system, or transmitted in any form or by any means, electronic, mechanical, by photocopying, recording, or by any other means, without the written permission of the publisher.

Contents

A medieval religious woman holding
a book.

Introduction

The Life of Margaret of Oingt

Margaret of Oingt was born around 1240 into a noble family in the French Beaujolais region.[1] She entered a Carthusian convent, the charterhouse of Poleteins, probably before 1268.[2] She had two brothers and three sisters of whom one, Agnes, joined the same convent as Margaret. Traces of her native village still exist, but the family became extinct in the second half of the fourteenth century. In 1288 a document designates her as prioress of the charterhouse.[3] Her name also appears in her father's will in 1297 and again in 1300 when her mother leaves her a legacy. She died in 1310. She was never canonized, but she was venerated as blessed and until the French Revolution a popular cult was devoted to her.

The meager facts known about her life contrast sharply with the vivid image of an intelligent, generous and humorous woman that emerges from her writings. She was a visionary, a mystic, a writer of great talent; among the many Carthusian religious writers she was the only woman. At the same time, she was the prioress of a charterhouse that was beset by financial problems. These multiple roles, which Margaret combined into a harmonious

---

1 There is not much information on Margaret's life. My remarks here are based on the introduction to her works in the Duraffour edition and the entry "Marguérite d'Oingt" in the *Dictionnaire de spiritualité*, vol. 10, columns 340-43.

2 The first exact date at which we know that she is a nun is 1286, mentioned at the beginning of her *Meditations*. But by that time she probably had been in the convent for some time. As Micheline de Fontette points out, a woman had to enter a charterhouse before the age of twenty-eight in order to become a regular nun. See *Les Religieuses à l'âge classique du droit canon*, p. 87. Charterhouse is the name for Carthusian convents and monasteries.

3 In the Carthusian order the head of a convent or monastery had the title of prior or prioress, not abbot or abbess as in the other monastic orders. The prior of the first charterhouse which was called the Grande Chartreuse also functioned as the head of the entire order. In other monastic orders his title would be that of Abbot General. For more details on the Carthusians see below.

whole, will structure this introduction. We will begin with a consideration of the Carthusian order and women's place in it. Then some remarks on thirteenth-century piety and mysticism will situate Margaret's spirituality in the context of her time.

The Carthusian Order and the Question of Women

The Carthusian order was founded by Saint Bruno who was born at Cologne around 1030.[1] When he was chancellor of the cathedral at Reims, he was driven from the city by a certain Manasses who had usurped the archbishop's place. Manasses was, according to the abbot Guibert of Nogent (1064-ca. 1125), a man of "great wickedness and senseless conduct."[2] Bruno, desiring a stricter and more ascetic way of life, went with some companions into a wild mountain region near Grenoble in southeastern France where he founded the first charterhouse. The ideals of the first Carthusians were penitence, poverty, humility, and obedience. Originally, Bruno had not intended to found a new order, but wanted to live by the original rule of Saint Benedict. In theory, Bruno's ideals were the ideals of most monastic orders, but some orders had become rich and powerful and had moved away from their original ideas. In the twelfth century Saint Bernard complained about the Benedictines:

> Look at their churches, glistening with gold while the poor are starving and naked outside.... Their object is to excite the devotion of the vulgar masses who are incapable of truly spiritual feelings.... But what kind of devotion do they produce? They do not bring men to prayer but tempt them into making offerings.[3]

The Carthusian order was characterized by its strict enforcement of the ideas of poverty and solitude, recalling the eremitic origins of monasticism, exemplified by its founder Saint Anthony (d. 356), one of the fathers of the early church who lived as a hermit in the desert. Guibert of Nogent describes the first charterhouse:

> The church there is not far from the foot of the mountain, in a little fold of its sloping side, and in it are thirteen monks who have a cloister quite suitable for common use but who do not live together in cloister

1 On his life see the entry by Bernard Bligny in the *New Catholic Encyclopedia*, vol. 2, 836-837.
2 Guibert wrote an extremely lively account of his times which has been translated in *Self and Society in Medieval France: The Memoirs of Abbot Guibert of Nogent*. The quote is on p. 59
3 Saint Bernard, *Apologia ad Guillelmum*, XII, 28. Cited by Jonathan Sumption in *Medieval Pilgrimage*, p. 155.

fashion like other monks. They all have their separate cells around the cloister, in which they work, sleep and eat.... They have water for both drinking and other purposes from a conduit, which goes around all their cells and flows into each through interior holes in the walls.... They hardly ever speak in any place, for when it is necessary to ask for anything, they do so by signs.... They wear hairshirts next to the skin and few other clothes.... Although they subject themselves to complete poverty, they are accumulating a very rich library.[1]

Originally the monks were even supposed to cook for themselves in their cells, but, as James Hogg found, "the do-it-yourself cooking was apparently unsuccessful."[2] Meat was strictly forbidden; fish (often the "gift of some good people," as Guibert remarked) was a common staple, as were vegetables, cereals, eggs, bread and cheese.

The extreme austerity of the order soon attracted many people in search of a purer life. Guibert speaks of men and women of all ranks as well as of children aged ten and eleven who in their way of thinking resembled old men and "mortified their flesh beyond the endurance of such tender years."[3]

Although documentation for Carthusian life is much more scarce than for some other orders, a fair amount of information can be found in the legislative collections, or statutes, that were issued by various Chapter Generals, as the meetings of the priors of the order were called. The first statutes were the *Consuetudines Cartusiae* (Carthusian customs), written as a letter around 1127 by Guigo I, the fifth prior of the Grande Chartreuse, the principal seat of the order. He stressed silence and solitude as the hallmarks of Carthusian life. Other important collections of statutes were the *Antiqua Statuta* (old statutes) of 1259, the *Nova Statuta* (new statutes) of 1368 and the *Tertia Compilatio* (third compilation) of 1509.[4]

The question of allowing nunneries to affiliate themselves with male orders was one of the thorniest in medieval monasticism. The

---

1   *Self and Society*, pp. 60-61. Since the copying of manuscripts was one of the foremost monastic occupations, the monks could build up their library rather quickly.

2   James Hogg, "Everyday Life in the Charterhouse in the Fourteenth and Fifteenth Centuries," p. 134. This study gives some very interesting details on the clothes, furniture (feather beds were forbidden), and even the shaving habits (originally six times a year, in the fifteenth century once a week) of the monks.

3   *Self and Society*, p. 62.

4   James Hogg, "Everyday Life," pp. 120-22.

cura monialum, or the care of the female religious, was troublesome and problematic, particularly in the areas of "pastoral care and economic maintenance". Since women were not allowed to say mass or hear confession, male priests had to come to the convent on a regular basis or even live there. On the whole, the monks tried to resist the incorporation or the affiliation of female branches of an order. In 1228, for example, the Cistercian order issued a statute "forbidding all further attachment of nunneries to the order and refusing the benefit of visitation and pastoral care to existing communities." The founders of the two great mendicant orders, Saint Francis and Saint Dominic, "refused in highly emotive terms to allow the general attachment of women to their orders."[1] An extreme expression of the monks' hostility toward women can be found in a declaration issued by a Premonstratensian monastery:

> Since nothing in this world resembles the evil of women and since the venom of the viper or the dragon is less harmful to men than their proximity, we hereby declare that for the good of our souls, our bodies and our wordly goods we will no longer accept sisters into our order and we will avoid them as we do mad dogs.

As Penny Schine Gold points out, "we thus see...in the Premonstratensian case the fear of women and their sexual temptation as one of the causes of the order's abandonment of women."[2]

Nevertheless, some women managed to join mendicant orders. Thus Saint Clare and her followers, the "Poor Clares", attached themselves to the Franciscans in 1212, and the Dominicans as well finally yielded to the pressures of the nuns: between 1245 and 1250 no fewer than thirty-two convents were incorporated in Germany alone. Through the authority of the pope the orders were forced to

---

1   The mendicant orders were all founded in the early thirteenth century. They are the Augustinians, the Carmelites, the Franciscans and the Dominicans. The name comes from Latin *mendicare* (=to beg) and signifies that these orders believed in poverty which meant that they were begging for their food. They thus imitated the poverty Jesus Christ had advocated. They could preach and hear confession and were generally not attached permanently to one monastery. On the *cura monialum* see Brenda M. Bolton, "Mulieres Sanctae," p. 141. The three quotes come from p. p,141, 143 and p. 151 respectively.

2   The Premonstratensian order had been founded by Norbert of Xanten in 1120. (It was named after Prémontré, located near Laon in France.) Originally receptive toward women, the order soon isolated them. On the acceptance/rejection pattern of female religious in many orders see Gold, *The Lady and the Virgin*, chap. 3. For the quote condemning women see Shulamith Shahar, *The Fourth Estate*, p. 36 and Gold, p. 88. The quote by Gold is from p. 88 as well.

do exactly the opposite of what their founders Saint Francis and Saint Dominic had desired.[1] The female branches of the mendicant orders, especially in Germany, played an important role in the development of mysticism and mystical writing.

Unlike the mendicant orders, the Carthusian order did not believe that its members should engage in public preaching or go begging in the streets. They had a strong ideal of seclusion and solitude (most of them would have preferred to live in a kind of desert or in a wild region like that of the original Chartreuse) and were reluctant even to consider any kind of female affiliation lest this solitude should be disturbed. The first nunnery to attach itself to the Carthusian order, the convent of Prébayon in Provence, must therefore have been quite insistent, because the nuns were ultimately successful. Founded in 610 by a relative of Saint Radegonde of Poitiers, this nunnery had lived by the first rule written for women, that of Caesarius of Arles which had a strong eremitic, that is reclusive, bent. Around 1140 the nuns showed a desire to adopt the Carthusian rule, with stricter rules of enclosure (or life in a cell) than that of Caesarius. The blessed John of Spain, prior of the charterhouse at Montrieux, adapted the *Consuetudines* of Guigo for them.

The development of the order's organization highlights some of the power struggles between male and female religious. At the beginning, the prioress alone was responsible for all aspects of convent life; but she did not represent her charterhouse at the Chapter General (this representation generally signaled the official affiliation of a given charterhouse), although she pledged obedience to the Chapter. The link between the Chapter and the charterhouse was a visitor, sent to the convent from time to time. There were some male clerics to take care of matters outside of the convent. In 1260 the Chapter General decided that a prior should henceforth be the head of the nuns. This decision caused some outrage and Prébayon seceded from the order in protest. Other female charterhouses relented only when the prior was renamed vicar and his authority was somewhat curtailed.[2] The vicar was the sole priest and confessor and regulated together with the prioress the nuns' correspondence with the outside world.[3] His position vis-à-vis the female religious was problematic, as we will see in one of Margaret's tales at the end of her writings.

---

1 Bolton, p. 153; p. 151.
2 See de Fontette, *Les Religieuses à l'âge classique du droit canon*, pp. 83-84.
3 Suzanne Fonay Wemple, "Women's Religious Orders: Carthusians," *Dictionary of the Middle Ages*, vol. 12, p. 687.

How can we imagine the life of Carthusian nuns? There were three classes of nuns: the regular nuns, the "converted" and the "given." A prospective nun had to bring a dowry to the convent, which meant that women of the poorer classes were excluded from becoming a full-fledged nun—a situation that existed in the other orders as well. The nuns wore a white wool habit with a scapular, a wimple with ribbons which covered the neck and a veil that could be moved forwards or backwards. Most of the manual labor was done by the "converted;" the nuns helped with the laundry, but of course could not do any work for gain. The strict enclosure forbade outside contact and "an ordinance of 1299 laid down that the nuns might only speak with strangers through a grill in the presence of two other members of the community."[1]

Carthusian nuns were consecrated differently than nuns in other orders. When they joined the order they received—in addition to the veil and the ring common to most orders—a stole and the maniple, a eucharistic vestment consisting of a strip of fabric carried on the left arm. They also received a benediction, or blessing, as deaconesses.[2] Consecrated nuns were allowed to read from the gospels at the evening office. One can imagine that women who were capable of reading Latin and of running their own affairs in the charterhouse began asking themselves why they could not say mass. And indeed, the *Nova Statuta* of 1368 accused women of having the audacity to desire just that. The mystical experiences of religious women at that time must be seen in this context. The women's visions often featured Eucharistic imagery, focusing on the transformation of the host into Christ's flesh and of wine into Christ's blood. Caroline Bynum has suggested that these visions provided a kind of authority that could substitute for the priestly privilege of celebrating mass and consecrating the host.[3] In Margaret's visions and in those of Beatrice of Ornacieux described by Margaret, the Eucharist, that is the sacrament of communion featuring consecrated bread and wine, and a fantastic image of the Holy Scriptures play important roles. Like many other mystical women, Margaret and Beatrice assumed functions in their visions that were denied to them in real life.

---

1 James Hogg, "Everyday Life in the Charterhouse," p. 143. For the different classes of nuns and their clothing see de Fontette, pp. 86-87.

2 De Fontette, p. 89. The deaconess figured in the early church. In the third century, for example, deaconesses could assist in the baptism of women and visit sick women for religious instruction. See Shahar, *The Fourth Estate*, p. 23.

3 Caroline Walker Bynum, *Jesus as Mother*, ch. 5 "Women Mystics in the Thirteenth Century: The Case of the Nuns of Helfta," pp. 170-262. We will return to this idea below.

Female Piety, Mysticism and Religious Writing

The religious possibilities open to women in the thirteenth century were shaped to a certain extent by developments that were not necessarily religious. The urbanization of Europe was an important factor in redefining ideas of piety and sanctity. While earlier saints had been found mostly among the ruling classes, the thirteenth century increasingly saw lay saints (i.e., not members of religious orders) from the middle class, such as merchants, that followed a trade and were married.[1] Ideas of sainthood and piety became more diverse, new needs arose, including the need for more religious texts in the vernacular. People "wanted desperately to hear the word of God and they longed to see true piety and evangelical poverty. This need gave rise to new religious orders of mendicant friars."[2] But given the strict rules regarding virginity and chastity in the monastery and the convent, pious lay people had to find other outlets for their religious fervor. In response to the laity's increased desire for a religious life, the mendicant orders created a "third order," whose members were called tertiaries. They could wear the habit and, under priestly guidance, follow the rules of the order, but they could continue to live in the world, although many of them lived in religious communities. The thirteenth century also saw the rise of the Beguine movement which was concentrated in the urban areas of Belgium, the Rhineland, and northern and southern France.[3] The Beguines, pious women who practiced active charity, were granted privileges by urban authorities, not the church. They had no uniform organization and hierarchy. They often practiced trades and, because they were exempted from taxes, were seen as competition by certain guilds.

Mystics could be found among the tertiaries as well as among the Beguines. Prominent Beguine mystics were Marie of Oignies (d. 1213) and Margaret Porete. But while the former remained within the realm of orthodoxy, the latter was burned in 1310 for her *Mirror of Simple Souls*, supposedly a heretical treatise. The

---

1 Cf. André Vauchez, "Lay People's Sanctity in Western Europe,"to appear in *Images of Sainthood in Medieval Europe*, ed. R. Blumenfeld-Kosinski and Timea Szell (Cornell University Press, 1991).
2 James A. Weisheipl in Szarmach, ed., *Introduction to the Medieval Mystics*, p. 138. For an explanation of the term "mendicant" see p. 4, note 1.
3 Shahar, *The Fourth Estate*, p. 52. The most comprehensive work on the Beguines and their male counterparts, the Beghards, is E.W. McDonnell, *The Beguines and Beghards in Medieval Culture*.

Mirror was written in French, not Latin, as most religious works were at that time. As Shulamith Shahar observes, "some Beguines engaged in translating the Holy Scripture into German and French and composed exegeses in the wake of translations, this being totally prohibited by Church authorities."[1] Eventually the Beguines were persecuted by the Inquisition: their voluntary poverty, mystical experiences—and undoubtedly their being women—had made them suspect and finally unacceptable.

Mystical visions and writing in the vernacular also characterized the Dominican nuns of the thirteenth century. The use of the vernacular in religious writings was often seen as a threat to the established church because it could devalue the mediating function of the priest. If the "illiterate"—as people who did not know Latin were called in the Middle Ages—could have direct access to and even compose religious works, certain aspects of the priest's role may become unnecessary. In 1210 a synod in Paris had explicitly forbidden the translation into French of theological books (except saints' lives)—infractions against this rule would be considered heresy. Nevertheless, the development of a vernacular religious literature could not be stopped. It was favored by the specific conditions in the thirteenth-century Germany Dominican nunneries where there were many learned women capable of translating Latin texts for their less educated sisters. Since the Dominicans saw themselves as a "preaching order," they were obliged to make their preaching accessible to everyone in their order, including women. In addition, the large number of mystics among Dominican women led to the production of visionary texts in German. The conditions in France were not the same as in Germany, but there as well—especially in the South—vernacular religious texts were written.[2]

Margaret of Oingt exemplifies these developments perfectly: she wrote in both Latin and Francoprovençal, her native dialect spoken in the region around Lyons. Religious women like the German Dominican nuns, the Beguine Margaret Porete and our Margaret of Oingt thus were responsible for very important literary innovations in the thirteenth and fourteenth centuries.

***

1 *The Fourth Estate*, p. 54. Exegesis, or interpretation of the Scriptures, was a privilege of the clergy.

2 For an important evaluation of the Dominican women's role in the development of vernacular literature see Herbert Grundmann, *Religiöse Bewegungen im Mittelalter*, pp. 452-75. I basically follow his thesis.

Much of the literary production at the time dealt with mystical experiences. The most basic definition of mysticism is a direct approach to God based on sensory perceptions, not on reason. Meditations, such as the ones offered by Margaret, often played a role in preparing the soul for the "mystical ascent," the steps that would allow a human being to move closer and closer to God. The soul would first be purified (this stage is called the purgative way), then feel illuminated with the love and knowledge of God (the illuminative way) and eventually feel God present in it: the soul, in a kind of spiritual marriage, is united with God (*unio mystica*). This state is often followed by "the dark night of the soul," a state of seeming abandonment by God. As we will see, Beatrice of Ornacieux, the subject of Margaret's *Life*, went through long periods of God's apparent absence which she endured without despair.

The mystical experience allowed the visionary "extraordinary glimpses of spiritual or otherwise hidden realities." For Master Eckhart (ca. 1260-1327), one of the great German mystics, a vision was an immediate experience of God which was prepared through asceticism and found its fulfillment in ecstasy.[1] Saint Augustin, in the fourth century, had spoken of three kinds of visions: the physical, the imaginative and the spiritual. An example of the first type is God's appearing to Moses on Mount Sinai; Saint Peter and Saint John had imaginative visions (for example, the apocalyptic vision recounted by Saint John in the book of Revelation); Saint Paul's rapture described in 2. Corinthians 12 would be termed a spiritual vision. For Augustine, all three types of visions allowed for a true revelation of God. Master Eckhart, on the other hand, devalued the first two types: for him only those visions that were totally beyond matter, that were intellectually and spiritually pure, were valid.[2] Most important, Master Eckhart associated the inferior types of visions with female mystics. Thus the emotive and affective sides of female mysticism that find their poetic expression in the German *Nonnenviten* (lives of nuns) and in texts like Margaret Porete's *Mirror of Simple Souls* as well as in the writings of Margaret of Oingt were seen by Eckhart as second best. Jacques de Vitry, the biographer of Marie of Oignies, described the ecstasy of mystical union: "They melted altogether in wondrous love for God until it seemed that they bowed under the burden of desire

---

1   Kieckhefer, *Unquiet Souls*, p. 151. For Master Eckhart see Otto Langer, *Mystische Erfahrung und Spirituelle Theologie*, p. 212.
2   Langer, p. 222.

and for many years they did not leave their beds except on rare occasions...Resting in tranquillity with the master...."[1]

But not all visions emphasized the passivity of rapturous love; visions were also prophecy and could bestow on a woman a status which she could never obtain by ordinary means. In the twelfth century Bernard of Clairvaux wrote to the mystic Hildegard of Bingen, extolling the divine grace and the hidden knowledge of God she had received through her visions. In the next century, Thomas Aquinas insisted that prophecy was a divine gift, not a sacrament. Thus he recognized the power and validity of the visions, but at the same time he clearly denied any priestly aspirations to the female recipients of prophetic visions.[2]

Simone de Beauvoir dismissed the female medieval mystics because of their "excessive sentimentalism, sometimes bordering on hysteria...and their narcissism."[3] Indeed, the visions recorded by thirteenth and fourteenth century religious women or their biographers are filled with strong emotions and imagery, much of it nuptial and erotic. In the *Life of Christina of Markyate* (late twelfth century) we find the following description of Christina as Christ's spouse: "She was rapt in ecstasy and saw herself in the presence of her savior: and she saw him whom she loved above all others, encircled with her arms and held closely to her breast."[4] Mechthild of Magdeburg (d. 1281), first a Beguine, then a Cistercian nun, made her soul cry out:

> Ah, dearest Love, for how long
> Hast thou lain in wait for thee?

And Love answers:

> I hunted thee for my pleasure,
> I caught thee for my desire,
> I bound thee for my joy,
> Thy wounds have made us one,
> My cunning blows, me thine.[5]

---

1 Cited by Shahar, p. 59.
2 See Shahar, pp. 56-57.
3 *Le deuxième sexe*, ch. 24. Cited by Shahar, p. 61.
4 Cited by Eleanor McLaughlin, "Women, Power and the Pursuit of Holiness," p. 113.
5 Translated from *The Flowing Light of the Godhead* by Lucy Menzies. In Petroff, p. 214.

Mechthild also speaks glowingly of the Lord's desire for her. He sees her as as "His bed," as the "stream of His ardor;" she will cool the heat of His divinity, the longing of His humanity and the lust of the Holy Ghost. Beatrice of Ornacieux, in a manifestation of grace, sees the Lord coming to her "like a person who kissed her vigorously and lovingly."[1]

Is language like this a sublimation for the lack of sexual experience in these women's lives? Or is it rather the only way they had to express their absolute devotion to Christ and their ardent love for Him? Inspired by the erotic and nuptial imagery used in the *Song of Songs* and particularly in Bernard of Clairvaux's commentary on that text, male mystics, as well, expressed their spiritual love with extreme ardor. Thus Philip the Carthusian had written in the thirteenth century: "You are my beloved bridegroom, to you I give my virginity, you are my comely bridegroom. My heart yearns for you always. You are my beloved and my friend."[2] He is addressing himself to the Virgin Mary! But on the whole the imagery used by women, Mechthild in particular, is more extreme than that of their male counterparts; it expresses the nuptial contract a nun made when she entered a convent and took Christ as her bridegroom in the most emotive language possible.

The main themes that occur again and again in both male and female mystical writings are meditiations on the humanity of Christ, a devotion to the Passion, and to a certain extent the cult of the Virgin. What distinguishes female mystics is a stronger emphasis on the Eucharist. Visions of hell and the Last Judgment are quite common, as are horrible visions of temptation, usually involving the devil.

Some visions differed little over the centuries. For example, Theresa of Avila in the sixteenth century often saw a small black figure next to her bed who gnashed his teeth in anger because he could not corrupt her.[3] This creature closely resembles the devil that paraded all sorts of vile images in front of Beatrice of Ornacieux, the saint whose life Margaret wrote in the thirteenth century; of course, she as well resisted temptation. The devil was

---

1 For Mechthild, see Karlheinz Deschner, *Das Kreuz mit der Kirche*, p. 108. Deschner consistently ridicules the experiences of female mystics by applying modern standards. Especially his analysis of phallic imagery in Theresa of Avila's writings is only titillating, and he makes no effort to understand Theresa in her own time and circumstances. For Beatrice of Ornacieux see this translation of the *Life*, paragraph 45.
2 Cited from Philip's *Marienleben* (Life of Mary) by Shahar, *The Fourth Estate*, p. 62.
3 Deschner, p. 113.

a common fixture in the medieval imagination. As Jonathan Sumption points out, "in popular thinking, the Devil's organization and methods were a reflection of God's. He too had his twelve apostles of evil, his rites and his Church. Just as God lived in the righteous, so the Devil 'possessed' the sinful."[1] Hell, as well, was ever present in the medieval mind. Often, hell was seen as alternately burning hot and freezing cold. "Sulphurous eddies of flames mixed with freezing hail," is how a seventh-century hermit describes it.[2] While Margaret's vision of hell in her *Page of Meditations* cannot rival Dante's description of it in the *Inferno*, her images are nevertheless powerful and frightening.

Devotion to the Passion was another characteristic of thirteenth-century mysticism. Already in the eleventh century pilgrims to the Holy Land reacted emotionally to the places where Christ had suffered. The sight of the Pillar of Pilate evoked in one pilgrim "the spitting, the smiting, the mocking, and the crown of thorns. Then on the place of Calvary, he passed through his mind an image of the Saviour crucified, pierced with a lance, reviled and mocked by all around him, crying out with a loud voice, and yielding up his spirit."[3]

The reenactment of Christ's sufferings became more systematic later on with the composition of the *Meditations of the Life of Christ*, written in Italy around Margaret's time, and depictions of the so-called *arma Christi*, the "weapons" He used in His sufferings. They consisted among others of pictures of nails, pincers, a hammer, a scourge, a lance, a ladder, a crown of thorns, and even Christ's footprints; each element would call forth a separate prayer or meditation. Some of Margaret's meditations directly reflect these spiritual patterns. A very striking example can be found in one of her letters:

> At noon, I reflected how my sweet Lord was tormented for our sins and suspended all naked from the cross between two thieves. When I came to the point where the evil people had deserted Him, I went towards Him with great respect, and removed the nails; then I took

1 *Medieval Pilgrimage*, p. 17.
2 Sumption, p. 20.
3 Sumption, p. 92.

Him upon my shoulders and took Him down from the
cross and put Him in the arms of my heart.[1]
With this kind of step-by-step recreation of the Passion and her
direct participation in it (she *enters* the scene) Margaret exemplifies and at the same time expands the possiblities of spiritual
expression in her time.

The same can be said for the devotion to the Eucharist which
emerges most clearly and dramatically in Margaret's *Life of
Beatrice of Ornacieux*. Caroline Bynum stresses the particularly
female emphasis on the Eucharist in the thirteenth century: "The
feast of *Corpus Christi* was championed by Juliana of Cornillon.
Mary of Oignies (+1213), Margaret of Ypres (+1237), and Christina
Mirabilis (+1224) could not bear to be without the eucharist.
Lutgard of Aywières (+1246) took such pleasure in it that her
abbess once compelled her to omit it as a penance."[2] Often the
devotion to the Eucharist took the form of an obsession: certain
women wanted to take communion many times a day. In other
cases, apparitions were associated with the Eucharist:

Christina Ebner sometimes saw Christ in human form
in the hands of the celebrant. Jane Mary of Maillé, too,
had a vision when a priest elevated the host at one mass:
she saw a small child with wounds in his side, hands,
and feet with blood gushing out of various parts of his
body.[3].

Some saintly women experienced the transformation of the host
physically: "When Jane Mary of Maillé was lying ill, she prayed
that she might take a drink from the priest's chalice, and suddenly
she found her mouth filled with blood."[4] Others were unable to
swallow the host. Beatrice of Ornacieux had a horrible experience
of this kind when one day after much hesitation she took communion and found herself with a growing lump of raw flesh in her
mouth! This phenomenon, known as *globus hystericus*, is linked

---

1 For the *Meditations*, an extremely popular text falsely attributed to Saint Bonaventure,
   see Richard Kieckhefer, *Unquiet Souls*, pp. 100-102. For the *arma Christi* see the
   interesting article by Elisabeth Vavra on the interaction between pictorial representations
   and visions "Bildmotiv und Frauenmystik: Funktion und Rezeption," pp. 201-230 in
   Dinzelbacher and Bauer, eds. *Frauenmystik im Mittelalter*, p. 226 and Kieckhefer, p. 111.
   Margaret's text is paragraph 130 of "Letters and Stories" in this translation.
2 *Jesus as Mother*, pp. 256-57.
3 Kieckhefer, *Unquiet Souls*, p. 171
4 Kieckhefer, p. 171.

by Caroline Bynum to hysteria or acute anxiety.[1] This diagnosis certainly fits Beatrice's case, since she agonized so much about whether she was worthy of the Eucharist that day that she almost fainted. Or take Dorothy of Montau in the fourteenth century:

> The richest mystical imagery is eucharistic: when she received communion, Christ "held a great banquet" in her soul, or "killed a fatted calf" within her, or kissed her soul and embraced it, or bore himself wihin her, or else she gave birth to him.[2]

These intense experiences of the Eucharist reflect the central position it occupied in religious women's lives. Picturing communion as a direct, powerful and loving contact with Christ allowed women to assume through their visions the priestly role they could not hold in real life. The same is true for visions and special religious experience in general.

Medieval women had few possibilities of transcending their predestined roles of wife and mother. Dorothy of Montau, whose Eucharistic imagery we just discussed, is a striking example of the empowerment afforded by a religious vocation. At age sixteen she had married a man well above forty. Within fourteen years she gave birth to nine children of whom eight quickly died. Although her husband loved her (according to Dorothy), he beat her and sometimes even put her in chains; he never approved of her religious fervor, although he accompanied her on several ill-fated pilgrimages. She finally found the courage to go alone on a pilgrimage to Rome, and during her absence her husband died. Thus liberated, she embarked on a life of extensive travel (more pilgrimages) and eventually of anchoritic devotion as a total recluse in a cell off the cathedral in the town of Marienwerder.[3] What Siegfried Ringler says about the fourteenth-century mystic Christina Ebner holds true for most of the women we have encountered in the introduction and particularly for Margaret of Oingt:

> Had she been a married women of the patrician bourgeoisie of Nuremberg, she would never have had the possibility of leading her own life, to have some literary

---

1 See *Holy Feast and Holy Fast*, p. 203. For the story, see paragraphs 88-93 of this translation of the *Life of Beatrice of Ornacieux*.

2 Kieckhefer, *Unquiet Souls*, p. 29.

3 See Siegfried Ringler, "Die Rezeption mittelalterlicher Frauenmystik als wissenschaftliches Problem, dargestellt am Werk der Christina Ebner," in Dinzelbacher and Bauer, eds., pp. 196- 97, and Kieckhefer, *Unquiet Souls*, pp. 22-33 for a detailed account of her life and piety.

activity, to influence the ecclesiastic and perhaps also the political events of her time. The emperor would never had kneeled before her. Religious aspirations, life in the cloister, asceticism: do they really represent limitations and the suppression of natural urges and instincts or rather attempts at self-realization? Where else did fourteenth-century women have comparable possiblities of taking charge of their own lives?[1]
Without diminishing the austerity and the restrictions of life in the convent, we can say that it was a place in which women had more autonomy and control over their own destiny than in secular life. A strong and self-assured voice like Margaret's was not heard in secular literature until Christine de Pizan (1365-1430?) who radically redefined what women could do in the realm of literature.

The Writings of Margaret of Oingt

Unlike some other mystical writers, Margaret did not initially intend her writings for a wide public. In fact, she did not dare write down her visions until she had consulted one of her trusted advisors, a prior named Hugues of Amplepuis. He submitted the account of her visions to the Chapter General of 1294 which considered them orthodox and approved them. With the danger of heresy looming large (we saw that Margaret's contemporary, Margaret Porete, was burned as a heretic), such caution becomes understandable. Once she had the approval of the Chapter, Margaret continued to write in a variety of languages and forms. Her texts were collected after her death in a manuscript that still exists under the number 5785R in the municipal library of Grenoble.[2] Someone added the account of three miracles that Margaret performed after her death.

The first text, the *Page of Meditations*, is the only one written in Latin. It has two quite different themes: love and fear. The first meditation, triggered by the singing of a psalm, deals with Margaret's thoughts about sin and salvation. Prayer and confession create the right atmosphere for the composition of the meditations: she feels compelled by a great force to write in order to commemorate the grace she has received. Margaret insists that God's love is all-encompassing; He is her family and He has made

---

1   "Die Rezeption," p. 197.
2   Two other manuscripts exist, but they date from the seventeenth century. For this translation I worked with a microfilm of manuscript 5785R and the excellent edition of Duraffour, Gardette and Durdilly. For information on the different manuscripts see that edition, pp. 15-23.

her in His likeness. Margaret's thoughts revolve around God's Incarnation, the Passion suffered by Jesus Christ and Mary's anguish. Jesus is compared to a tradesman who redeemed the world at a high price; to a physician who healed the world at a high cost. In a striking depiction of the pain of childbirth Margaret compares Christ's sufferings on the cross to an endless and painful ordeal of labor. If Margaret could only suffer as much! She even would become a leper, if this could express her love for Christ. She ardently desires her death: it would bring her closer to Christ.

In paragraph 64 the tone changes. Margaret meditates on the evil ways of humanity. She does not spare the religious; on the contrary, they who should set an example, are lax and malicious. Her complaints sound as if she had specific people in mind, probably some nuns in her charterhouse. These thoughts lead her to a meditation on death and the Last Judgment: More swiftly than a race horse or an eagle will those rush to hell who do not keep God's commandments. They will be dragged by devils into the pit of hell where their breasts and lips will be gnawed by horrible creatures. They will lie on burning coals, be trapped in bubbling cauldrons and wear tunics of black pitch which, when removed, will tear off their flesh. Hunger, thirst, and hatred for each other will torment them forever. But those who followed God's word will be part of the new world that God will create. Unspeakable joys and delights await the elect in the new Jerusalem.

These images make Margaret think about her own life and how grateful she is to Christ that He protected her from the multiple perils of the world: the flesh and the devil. "Write into my heart," she concludes, "what you want me to do."

The second text, the *Mirror*, tells in three chapters of a magnificent vision a "person of Margaret's acquaintance," that is, Margaret herself, experienced.[1] Christ appears to her, holding a closed book in His hand, a motif that is common in the church sculpture of Margaret's time. On the book's cover she sees white, black and red letters; the clasps have golden letters. The white letters contain the life of Christ; the black letters the ignominies

---

1 This method of presenting visions dates back at least to the New Testament where Saint Paul says in 2. Corinthians 12:2: "I know a man in Christ who fourteen years ago was caught up to the third heaven—whether in the body or out of the body I do not know." And then in verse 7 he reveals that it was he himself who had this vision: "In view of the extraordinary nature of these revelations, to stop me from getting too proud I was given a thorn in the flesh...." Margery Kempe (1373-1439) introduces her first vision by saying "When this creature was twenty years old...," meaning herself. (*The Book of Margery Kempe*, transl. Susan Dickman. In Petroff, p. 314.)

He suffered at the hands of the Jews; and in the red letters Margaret sees His wounds and blood. The clasps have words from the Bible on them. Margaret then meditates on these themes and asks herself how she can imitate Christ's sufferings. In Chapter 2, the book opens, revealing—like a mirror—a "delightful place," the origin of all goodness. This vision leads Margaret to meditate on heaven, the angels and the saints. In Chapter 3, the book plays no role: here Margaret tells of a glorious body in which she can see herself as in a mirror. Again, she takes this vision as the basis for a meditation, this time on God's goodness, beauty and strength. But some people—like pigs—prefer the mire to God's beauty. The *Mirror* ends with a prayer: may God give us purity so that we will be able to see His glorious face after our deaths.

The third text is a saint's life, the *Life of the Virgin Saint Beatrice of Ornacieux*. Beatrice, who died in 1303, was a nun in the charterhouse of Parmenie. There is some speculation that Margaret may have been her teacher when she was a novice.[1] Margaret opens the *Life* in a traditional way: like all saints' lives, it is written in God's honor. The function of a saint's live is to set an example; according to Jacques de Vitry, such a text should "strengthen the faith of the weak, instruct the unlettered, incite the indolent, provoke the devout to imitation and confute the rebellious and the unbelievers."[2] And this is exactly what Margaret sets out to do. She tells how, at a young age, Beatrice left the world to devote herself to her spiritual life. She was virtuous and received many graces. The many tears she shed almost cost her her eyesight.[3] Nails that pierced her hands drew only water, not blood. She defended herself against the attacks of the devil with severe acts of penance "which were sometimes immoderate," as Margaret tellingly adds. In Chapter 2, Beatrice is finally freed from the devil's temptations by the Virgin. She expresses a strong desire for death. Chapter 3 opens with a vision in which Christ tells her in an unspeakably sweet voice not to desire illness or death. Beatrice now realizes that these desires had conflicted with her service of the Lord. In Chapter 4 Margaret recounts Beatrice's great vision of a glorious multitude of people carrying Christ's body. In Chapter 5, her spirit travels to the saints in paradise while her body

---

1 See the informative note on p. 161 of the Duraffour edition.
2 Jacques de Vitry, the author of the important *Life of Marie of Oignies*, offered this definition in a letter to Foulques of Toulouse. Cited by Michael Goodich in "The Contours of Female Piety in Later Medieval Hagiography," p. 32.
3 Copious tears were a sign of holiness. Jacques de Vitry tells how Marie of Oignies had to wring out her veil many times a day because it was soaked with tears.

remains in bed and can even be seen by her spirit—a most interesting description of the visionary experience. Beatrice never revealed the details of this vision. Chapter 6 contains a splendid Eucharistic vision where Beatrice sees the host as a little child surrounded by a multi-colored brightness which represents the Trinity. The next Chapter recounts the experience we described above: Beatrice's inability to swallow the host, transformed into a lump of flesh. Only an ardent prayer and subsequent fainting spell allow her to finally swallow it. Chapter 8 contains many indescribable visions, while Chapter 9 (chronologically situated after Beatrice's death) features the picturesque and rather amusing account of the trials and tribulations of a vicar whom some nuns ordered to go from Eymeux to Parmenie to retrieve the bones of Beatrice and two other saintly women. A prayer to the Virgin miraculously lowered a storm-swollen mountain stream so that the vicar and his precious load could cross. Another miracle tells of Beatrice's walking through a closed door to join her companions in prayer.

The fourth part of Margaret's writing consists of her letters and some stories. The first letter contains a meditation on the Passion and the most erotic image Margaret uses in all her writings to express her love of Christ. The second letter responds to some inquiries of her unknown correspondent. Here she insists on the curative powers of writing.[1] She also speaks of her problems as prioress: a late harvest, the church in bad repair and so forth. The next two letters recount various visions, including a stunning one of a deserted landscape with an inverted tree.[2] She also saw a gate with precious stones, the gate being of course Jesus Christ.

The stories that follow the letters recount a prophetic vision Margaret had of the death of archbishop Henri of Villars as well as the miraculous knowledge Margaret had of a missing skull in a churchyard.[3] The last story is very touching. Dom Durand had asked for a favor from Margaret. She promises one for the next time he will see her; after her death Margaret appears to him in

---

1   The theme of writing in Margaret's thought will be the subject of the interpretive essay.

2   According to Roland Maisonneuve, such a tree also appears in Hindu symbolism, esoteric Hebrew writings, in Islam and in Icelandic and Finnish folklore. See "L'Expérience mystique et visionnaire de Marguérite d'Oingt," p. 94.

3   Richard Kieckhefer shows the importance of prophetic visions in *Unquiet Souls*: "A further variety of revelation, sometimes linked with rapture and sometimes not, is what late medieval sources refer to as prophecy: preternatural knowledge of future, distant, or secret affairs.... Like other forms of revelation...it was an extraordinary sign of divine favor, indicating privileged contact with its divine source" (p. 161). See pp. 161-65 for some fascinating stories of prophetic visions.

the form of a white dove and brings him the greatest sweetness he had ever known: a beautiful last glimpse of this extraordinary woman.

A fifteenth-century rendering of the Grande Chartreuse, the first charterhouse of the Carthusian Order. In realaity, it was a simple stone building in the mountain wilderness.

Bibliography

Primary Sources

Manuscript 5785 R, Municipal Library of Grenoble.

Les Oeuvres de Marguérite d'Oingt. Publiées par Antonin Duraffour, Pierre Gardette and Paulette Durdilly. Paris: Société d'Edition "Les Belles Lettres," 1965.

Petroff, Elizabeth Alvilda, ed. *Medieval Women's Visionary Literature*. New York, Oxford: Oxford University Press, 1986.

Wilson, Katharina, ed. *Medieval Women Writers*. Athens, GA: University of Georgia Press, 1984.

Secondary Sources

Baker, Derek, ed. *Medieval Women*. Oxford: Blackwell, 1978.

Bowman, May Ann. *Western Mystics: A Guide to the Basic Works*. Chicago: American Library Association, 1978.

Bynum, Caroline Walker. *Jesus as Mother. Studies in the Spirituality of the High Middle Ages*. Berkeley and Los Angeles: The University of California Press, 1982.

---------. *Holy Feast and Holy Fast. The Religious Significance of Food to Medieval Women*. Berkeley, Los Angeles: University of California Press, 1987.

Deschner, Karlheinz. *Das Kreuz mit der Kirche: Eine Sexualgeschichte des Christentums*. Munich: Wilhelm Heyne Verlag, 1974.

Dinzelbacher, Peter and Dieter R. Bauer, eds. *Frauenmystik im Mittelalter*. Ostfildern: Schwabenverlag, 1985.

Dronke, Peter. *Women Writers of the Middle Ages: A Critical Study of Texts from Perpetua (+203) to Marguérite Porete (+1310)*. Cambridge: Cambridge University Press, 1984.

Fontette, Micheline de. "La Naissance des moniales chartreuses." *Analecta cartusiana* 56 (1981).

---------. *Les Religieuses à l'âge classique du droit canon*. Paris: Vrin, 1967.

Gaillard, Bernard. "Marguérite d'Oingt." In *Dictionnaire de la spiritualité*. Vol. 10, columns 340-43.

Gold, Penny Schine. *The Lady and the Virgin: Image, Attitude, and Experience in Twelfth-Century France*. Chicago and London: University of Chicago Press, 1985.

Goodich, Michael. "The Contours of Female Piety in Later Medieval Hagiography," *Church History* 50 (1981): 20-32.

Grundmann, Herbert. *Religiöse Bewegungen im Mittelalter*. Berlin: Emil Ebering, 1935. (Pp. 452-475 on "The religious women's movement and vernacular literature".)

Guibert of Nogent. *Self and Society in Medieval France: The Memoirs of Abbot Guibert of Nogent* (1064-ca.1125). Edited with an introduction and notes by John F. Benton. New York: Harper and Row, 1970.

Haug, Walter. "Zur Grundlegung einer Theorie mystischen Sprechens." Pp. 494-508 in Kurt Ruh, ed. *Abendländische Mystik im Mittelalter.*

Hogg, James. "Everyday Life in the Charterhouse in the Fourteenth and Fifteenth Centuries." Pp. 113-46 in M. Heinrich Appelt, ed. *Klösterliche Sachkultur des Spätmittelalters.* Vienna: Österreichische Akademie der Wissenschaften, 1980.

Kieckhefer, Richard. *Unquiet Souls: Fourteenth-Century Saints and Their Religious Milieu.* Chicago: University of Chicago Press, 1984.

Langer, Otto. *Mystische Erfahrung und Spirituelle Theologie: Zu Meister Eckhart's Auseinandersetzung mit der Frauenfrömmigkeit seiner Zeit.* Munich and Zurich: Artemis Verlag, 1987.

McDonnell, Ernest W. *The Beguines and Beghards in Medieval Culture.* 1954. Rpt. New York: Octagon Books, 1969.

McNamara, Jo Ann and Suzanne Wemple. "Sanctity and Power: The Dual Pursuit of Medieval Women." Pp. 90-118 in Renate Bridenthal and Claudia Koonz, eds. *Becoming Visible. Women in European History.* Boston: Houghton Mifflin Company, 1977.

McLaughlin, Eleanor C. "Equality of Souls, Inequality of Sexes: Woman in Medieval Theology." Pp. 213-66 in Rosemary Radford Ruether, ed. *Religion and Sexism: Images of Woman in the Jewish and Christian Traditions.* New York: Simon and Schuster, 1974.

--------. "Women, Power and the Pursuit of Holiness in Medieval Christianity." Pp. 99-130 in Rosemary Ruether and Eleanor Mc-Laughlin, eds. *Women of Spirit: Female Leadership in the Jewish and Christian Traditions.* New York: Simon and Schuster, 1979.

Maisonneuve, Roland. "L'Expérience mystique et visionnaire de Marguérite d'Oingt." Pp. 81-102.In J. Hogg, ed. *Kartäusermystik und Mystiker.* Salzburg: Institut für Anglistik und Amerikanistik, Universität Salzburg, 1981.

Nichols, John A. and Lillian Thomas Shank, eds. *Medieval Religious Women, Volume 1: Distant Echoes.* Kalamazoo, Mich.: Cistercian Publications, 1984.

Parisse, Michel. *Les Nonnes au moyen âge.* Le Puy: Christine Bonneton, 1983.

Petry, Ray C. *Late Medieval Mysticism.* Philadelphia: Westminster Press, 1957.

Ringler, Siegfried. "Die Rezeption mittelalterlicher Frauenmystik als wissenschaftliches Problem." Pp. 178-200 in Dinzelbacher and Bauer, eds. *Frauenmystik im Mittelalter*.

Rothwell, W. "The Hours of the Day in Medieval French." *French Studies* 13 (1959): 240-51.

Ruh, Kurt, ed. *Abendländische Mystik im Mittelalter*. Stuttgart: Metzler, 1986.

Shahar, Shulamith. *The Fourth Estate*. Trans. Chaya Galai. London and New York: Methuen, 1983.

Sumption, Jonathan. *Pilgrimage: An Image of Medieval Religion*. Totowa, N.J.: Rowman and Littlefield, 1975.

Szarmach, Paul, ed. *An Introduction to the Medieval European Mystics*. Binghamton, N.Y.: State University of New York Press, 1984.

Underhill, Evelyn. *Mysticism*. 1911. New York: Dutton, 1961.

---------. *The Mystics of the Church*. New York: Schocken, 1964.

Vauchez, André. "Lay People's Sanctity in Western Europe: Evolution of a Pattern (12th and 13th Centuries)." In R. Blumenfeld-Kosinski and T. Szell, eds. *Images of Sainthood in Medieval Europe* (forthcoming at Cornell University Press, 1991).

Weinstein, Donald and Rudolph M. Bell. *Saints and Society: The Two Worlds of Western Christendom, 1000-1700*. Chicago: University of Chicago Press, 1982.

Wimsatt, J. "St. Bernard, the Canticle of Canticles, and Medieval Piety." Pp. 77-96 in Szarmach, ed. *An Introduction to the Medieval European Mystics*.

The Writings of Margaret of Oingt[1]

A Page of Meditations

1 In the year of our Lord 1286, on the Sunday of Septuagesima,[2] I Margaret, the maidservant of Christ, was in church at mass when, as an introduction to the mass, the following verse was being sung: "The sighs of death will surround me."[3] And I began to think about the misery to which we are consigned because of the sin of the first parents. And while thinking about this I began [to feel] such fear and such pain that my heart seemed to fail me completely, and because of this I did not know whether I was worthy of salvation or not. When I heard afterwards the introductory verse that David sung so sweetly to the Lord, "I love you, Lord etc.," my heart was completely relieved because I recalled the sweet promise the Lord makes His friends when He says: "I love those who love me,"[4] and because I knew that He is so good and so mild that He would never permit those who love Him to perish.

2. And after I considered the great sweetness and compassion which is in Him, filled with great pain, I threw myself down full length in front of His precious body and petitioned and prayed to Him humbly that He give me what He knows I need.

3. Then He, full of sweetness and gentleness, by His grace visited me without delay and gave me His sweet consolation and such a will to do good that it seemed to me that I was all changed and renewed. After that I got up and kneeled in front of the Lord and confessed to Him everything I could remember in which I may have offended Him and promised Him to amend myself now and hereafter.

---

1 All biblical references (also for Margaret's other texts) are to the Vulgate version of the Bible, that is, the version most commonly used in the Middle Ages. If the numbering is different in the Revised Standard Version it will be supplied in parentheses. Brackets in the text indicate that I added words for better comprehension. For easy reference the numbering of the paragraphs corresponds to that of the Duraffour edition in which the Latin text of the *Page of Meditations* is numbered separately, while all the other texts, written in Francoprovençal, are numbered consecutively. In the manuscript, the paragraphs are set off by an ornamental symbol but are not numbered.

2 This is the Sunday seventy days before Easter.

3 Psalm 17:5 (Psalm 18:4).

4 Proverbs 8:17.

4. I began to think about and to contemplate the sweetness and goodness which is in Him, and the great good He had done me and all of humanity. I was so full of these thoughts that I lost my appetite and my sleep. And I thought that I would either die or languish if I did not remove these thoughts from my heart, but I did not find it in my heart to remove them, because I found so much solace in them and because they brought all the means and things that can gladden man's heart in this world; and while contemplating Him there was nothing in my heart that did not come from my sweet creator. I thought that the hearts of men and women are so flighty that they can hardly ever remain in one place, and because of that I fixed in writing the thoughts that God had ordered into my heart so that I would not lose them when I removed them from my heart, and so that I could think them over little by little whenever God would give me His grace. And for that reason I ask all those who read this text not to think badly [of me] because I had the presumption to write this, since you must believe that I have no sense or learning with which I would know how to take these things from my heart, nor could I write this down without any other model[1] than the grace of God which is working within me. And indeed, as I remembered my sins, they all came into my innermost self in order, beginning with the hour in which I began to write this and up to the moment when I had put everything down in writing.

5. Now you will find out how I converted completely to Him and how I began to tell Him of my fasting; this is how I began to speak to Him: sweet Lord Jesus Christ, what should I do since the pains of death will surround me and the fear of your judgments will totally terrorize me; since the times are so dark that even if I exist today I do not know whether I will exist tomorrow and no one is cetain of his salvation. And I do not know whether you love me or not. Nevertheless, sweet Lord, I am certain that your words are good and true because you say that you love those who love you. And for that reason I assemble everything that I believe can bring me to love you.

6. Sweet Lord, it seems to me that nature requires man to love his parents, his brothers and sisters, his friends, his spouse and his benefactors. Oh sweet Creator, if I love my father who is a mortal man, how incomparably more must I love you who is my

---

1 The Latin word for "learning" is *clericatus* here which refers strictly speaking to the clerical office. But in Old French the term *clergie* denotes "clerkliness," that is, knowledge or learning, including the ability to read and write. Model (Lat. *exemplar*) is a term used in manuscript copying: it is the manuscript that one copies from.

spiritual father and my eternal life. But I am not worthy to call myself your daughter, for I have sinned toward you and your angels; but nonetheless, I know that you do not want the death of sinners but rather want them to convert and live. For that reason, and because I have no father or friend except for you, I come back to you.

7. My Lord God, dear God, do not be offended if I call you father, since you created me when I was nothing, and you made my soul and my body, and you made me in your image and likeness through your pity.

8. Sweet dear Lord, you are my brother; but it is very presumptuous of me to say this, since I am a small worm and you are so great and so worthy that all learned people who ever were and who will ever be do not know how to describe you or to think about you. Oh beautiful sweet Lord Jesus Christ, who gave me the audacity to speak of such marvellous things if not you who are the true God and my brother and who showed us the greatest love? Oh beautiful sweet Lord, how great was that love! Certainly it was so great that all the virtues of heaven and all the angels of paradise could not contain you; for that reason you descended to this world in order to assume our humanity.

9. Oh, how extremely mild and wonderful was that love! Never were there such great and marvellous things nor so many miracles done than those from which God came who was without beginning, nor will such miracles be done again as long as that lasts which will last forever. Oh God, what marvellous deeds were those that this love did! Certainly they were such that He who was so big that the whole world could not contain Him and who held the whole world in His hand, He, I say, is the one whom love drove to so much that He made Himself enter the body of a young girl, and from that He who was the true God made Himself a mortal human. And He who was the king of kings and the lord of lords, and He who created the heavens and all creatures who are meant to serve Him, I say, love drove Him to so much that He was made to serve man.

10. And Him, who was blessed in the food and the saintly refreshment of the glorious angels and who was such a great lord that His honor could not be destroyed nor His powers decrease, Him, I say, love drove to so much that He Himself did not have any bread to eat. He, who was sitting on the glorious throne as the true God which He was, and who was being served so honorably and with such great reverence by the glorious angels, certainly it was He whom love drove to so much that He had Himself thrown into a small manger between an ox and an ass, and made Himself suffer even worse things, since He was derided and [people] spit into His

face and many other vile things were done to Him which I can neither describe nor think about.

11. Oh, beautiful sweet Jesus Christ, your kindnesses are so many and so great that I cannot speak of them nor think of them. Oh blessed Creator, what shall I do and what advice will you give me since I am so deeply tormented? Oh most gentle Jesus Christ, what solace will I be able to have from you, since, when I contemplate and look at your kindnesses which are so numerous and so full of love, I believe that if the worst man in all the world contemplated and considered this well, he would be converted to you; and I, miserable and in pain, I do not know how to love you who nourished me and protected me from all perils starting at the hour of my birth! Because of this I have great fear since I do not see how else I could obtain your grace.

12. Sweet Lord, I do not know what else to do but to think about the grace and the kindnesses that you gave me. Oh, beautiful Lord God Jesus Christ, give me grace so that I can think and contemplate in this way, and so that I can acquire your saintly love.

13. Oh, most gentle Jesus Christ, the greatest love you showed me was when you wanted to hide away all your strength in my love! You who were so strong that in the strength of your arms you carried and supported the whole world, and so powerful that all in this world act according to your will; with a single word you can destroy and make perish the whole world and with another single word you can remake it better and more beautiful. Oh, beautiful Lord God, how did it come about that you suffered your strength to be so diminished that you allowed yourself to be captured, bound and led to those who wanted to destroy you and that you permitted yourself to be robbed and tied to a column as if you were a wild beast?

14. Oh, beautiful Lord God, you did not only hide your strength; indeed, you also wanted to hide your wisdom which was so great that through it you ordained these marvellous things which are in the heavens and the course of the sun, the moon and the stars; you made the days and the nights, time and hours, and ordained the course of the waters and you made the firmament of heaven and earth; and all this you ordained so firmly that never afterwards will anything change in any way.

15. You ordained the good weather and the rain and the cold and the heat; and all those who exist you made so wisely that they will never forget your command.

16. You were the master and the lord of all knowledge and the foremost counsel of the glorious angels. Oh, Lord God, what coun-

seled you to hide this marvellous knowledge if not the great love that you had for us?

17. Oh most gentle one, you made yourself into the likeness of a fool because of the great love you have for us, when you let the false Judas push you in front of him and betray you to your mortal enemies who treated you as if you were a fool by nature. These most unjust people covered up your saintly face and afterwards they struck you because of their great wickedness; and then they interrogated you and someone beat you in the most profound mockery. And in front of these worst people you were like a lamb being sheared, and not a single bad word came out of your saintly mouth.

18. Lord God Jesus Christ, when I think all this over carefully, my heart is all disturbed.

19. You were and are the true judge of all living and dead people and because of the great love you have for us, you suffered it that miserable people condemned you to death.

20. You were the greatest health and the true physician whose touch healed the sick and whose fragrance resuscitated the dead;[1] and for that reason, since you knew that we were infected by mortal sin which forced us to go to the pains of hell, you wanted to carry all our weariness and pain so that we could have perfect health; and you wanted to suffer the pain of death so that we could have the eternal life.

21. Sweet Lord Jesus Christ, you were the sun of justice and the splendor of eternal light; you were the mirror without stain into which the angels wanted to look and whose beauty amazed the sun and moon; you were the precious stone in which were all good virtues; you were so full of virtues that you healed all illnesses.

22. There is no such poor man in the world that, if he had you, would not become rich quickly; nor is there one so sad and sorrowful that, if he had you, would not be joyful and smiling; nor is there one so stupid and ignorant that, if he had this precious stone, would not immediately be wise and intelligent; and no person that carried it[2] could fall into the hands of his enemies. And there are so many good virtues that I cannot count them.

23. You are the sweet electuary[3] in which are all good flavors and of whose goodness live the holy souls in paradise.

---

1   Jesus as a physician is a common topic in medieval writings.
2   That is, the precious stone=Jesus.
3   A powdered medicine mixed with honey or other sweet substances.

24. Oh God, how precious is this place which is full of so many virtues and values that, whoever will be there, will never be ill and his life will last forever and he will never grow old nor lose his loveliness and beauty.

25. You are the glorious rose in which are all good odors and colors.

26. Your beauty is so great that all other beauties are nothing but wool rags compared to your beauty.

27. Oh, Lord God, now I see that there is nothing so precious and so valuable as the souls of men and women; and because you, who were the true Solomon who was full of wisdom and whose realm was all filled with the riches of paradise, because you knew how worthy were the holy souls whom you had made in your image and likeness, you wanted to act as a tradesman so that you could buy them and put a price on them so high that it is a blessed thing to speak and think about.

28. Oh, Lord God Jesus Christ, it was not enough for you to descend from heaven to earth where you suffered such disdain and disgrace; indeed, you wanted to spill all your precious blood for the great love that you have for us, and afterwards you wanted to suffer the most shameful death, which is death on the cross.

29. Sweet Jesus Christ, you loved us so much that because of the great love you had for our souls you lost all your beauty which was so great that a human heart cannot imagine it.

30. Oh, most precious and noble body, how blessed was it to contemplate you at the time of your Passion, when the unjust traitors had spat at your beautiful face so that you, who was beautiful above all else, seemed to be a leper. Oh, beautiful sweet lord, what bitter pain could the sweet mother feel who was present and thus knew you, she who had nourished and breastfed you, when she saw you die such a vile and unjust death. And surely every creature must suffer great pain who contemplates all this well and who then does not know how to love you with all his heart. And I, weary and miserable, what shall I do when I still do not know how to love you?

31. Sweet Lord Jesus Christ, my heart will never be in peace until I know how to love you from all my heart, and there is nothing in all this world that I desire as much as this.

32. Sweet lord, I left my father and my mother and my brothers and everything in this world for love of you, but this is much too little; since the riches of this world are nothing but sharp thorns, he who has more of them has more misfortune. And because of that it seems to me that I rejected nothing but misery and indigence;

but you know, sweet Lord, that if I had a thousand worlds and could take everything from them at my will, I would leave everything for love of you, and if you gave me whatever there is in heaven or on earth, I would not consider myself content unless I had you, for you are the life of my soul, and I have—nor do I want to have—no father and no mother except for you.

33. Are you not my mother and more than mother? The mother who bore me labored at my birth for one day or one night, but you, my sweet and lovely Lord, were in pain for me not just one day, but you were in labor for more than thirty years. Oh, sweet and lovely Lord, how bitterly were you in labor for me all through your life! But when the time approached where you had to give birth, the labor was such that your holy sweat was like drops of blood which poured out of your body onto the ground.[1]

34. And when the worst traitors made you a prisoner, one of them gave you such a blow that your face was left all black; and afterwards they began to mock you and bent their knees in front of you in pure mockery and greeted you by saying: hail, king of the Jews.

35. Oh, lovely Lord God, those could not get enough of your torments, and surely they showed this well when afterwards they tied you to a certain column where they whipped you so stretched out that it seemed that you were stripped of your skin, so covered with blood were you; and after they had whipped you, they put on your tender head a certain crown of thorns that pierced your vital parts and your eyes.

36. Oh, Sweet Lord Jesus Christ, who ever saw any mother suffer such a birth! But when the hour of the birth came you were placed on the hard bed of the cross where you could not move or turn around or stretch your limbs as someone who suffers such great pain should be able to do; and seeing this, they stretched you out and fixed you with nails and you were so stretched that there was no bone left that could still have been disjointed, and your nerves and all your veins were broken. And surely it was no wonder that your veins were broken when you gave birth to the world all in one day.

37. Oh, lovely Lord God, still you were not satisfied with all the pains that you had suffered; indeed, you suffered it that they pierced your side with a certain spear so cruelly that your whole kind body was split and pierced; and your precious blood gushed forth with such strength that the courtyard flowed with it like a

---

1   For the context of the idea of Jesus as mother see Bynum, *Jesus as Mother*, pp. 110-169.

large stream, and it gushed forth with such great abundance that it must have come from a truly great stretching.

38. Lord God, it was no wonder that the sword which pierced your body penetrated the soul of your glorious mother who so tenderly loved you.[1]

39. Oh, lovely Lord God, who ever saw at any other time that a mother wanted to die such a vile death for the love of her child? Surely, no one ever saw this, since your love was beyond all other loves.

40. Oh, lovely Lord God, how badly is your goodness received by us! You suffered cruel anguish without pity and beyond measure, and you did not find one who would know how to show recognition and gratefulness for such great pain.

41. Sweetest Lord, you were tormented by different tortures: you saw your loving disciples whom you loved so tenderly left behind as orphans; and they were filled with great pain because they were separated from you.

42. From elsewhere you saw your sweet mother who seemed to be dead because of the great anguish she suffered for your hard death, and I truly believe that you were as tormented by her pain as by your death.

43. Oh, Lord God, what was a greater pain than the one you suffered when you saw your disciples who had left you and who were so forsaken; or was it a greater pain when you saw your holy mother so forsaken and tormented; or were you more tormented than that when you were pierced by such a hard nail; or were you more tormented when you died such a vile death?

44. I truly believe that you would answer whoever interrogated you as follows: that all these pains were most grievous to you, but that there was one which surpassed all others and that was when you thought of the most vile death you died for the love of those still to come and who were, because of this, ungrateful towards you, and when you saw that you lost that which you had bought so dearly and which you loved so tenderly.

45. Sweet Lord, when I reflect well and contemplate your great pain when your creatures separate themselves from you, it seems to me that one of the things that pleases you most is when you see that your creature knows how to stay close to you and is converted to doing good.

---

1 Cf. Luke 2:35 where Simeon prophesies to Mary: "and a sword will pierce through your own soul also."

46. Sweet Lord, everything that you did for love of me and of the whole human race draws me towards loving you, but the memory of your most holy Passion makes me love you even more; therefore it seems to me, beautiful sweet Lord, that I found that which I had desired so much, that is, that I love nothing but you, or for yourself or for your love. And surely this is the moment, sweet Lord, since it seems to me that I love nothing but being with you.

47. Sweet Lord, what shall I do in that hour when I will not be able to help or take care of myself, when my mouth and eyes will be closed and my soul will be separated from the body? Then my enemies will be before and behind me; they will be so glittering that they will be able to tempt me. One will tempt me against the faith, another with vainglory, another will try to make me despair.

48. Sweet Lord, what shall I do and what will become of me in that terrible hour, that is, at my end and on the day of judgment? Sweet Lord, what shall I do then? In which hand will you place me, and in which place will you lodge me?

49. Sweet Lord, I beseech you and ask you because of your great mercy that you look at me in that hour with those benevolent eyes with which you looked at my master, the blessed Peter, and that you give me the protection of your holy faith and the sign of your holy Passion; and I entreat you that you give me such firm perseverance that I will be beyond all fear and all doubt.

50. And I beseech you, sweet dear Lord, that, as truly as I loved your sweet mother above everything else but you, it will be your will that she will be with me in that hour when my soul will part from the body, so that the devil will not be able to come near me.

51. And I beseech you that you give me virtue and grace in that hour so that I can invoke and call out to you and commend my soul to you as from a good heart; and I pray to you that you will receive it [the soul] through the hands of your holy angels.

52. And I beseech you, sweet lord, that you will not permit me to pass from this life before you have purified me completely.

53. Sweet Lord, I have no father or mother except for you, and you know that I love you from all my heart and that I desire nothing else but you.

54. Sweet Lord, it would be very bitter for me if, at the moment when I part from this misery in which I find myself, I had to go elsewhere but near you, however unworthy I may be. But I know well that you can make me worthy if you like.

55. Sweet Lord, I beseech you to give me suffering in this world just as you suffered for love of me, for I am ready to suffer whatever you may give me as long as I am with you.

56. Sweet Lord, if you want me to be despised and suffer persecution, I want it, too. If you want me to be a leper, I want that too rather than not to have you.[1] Or if you want me to be burned, drowned, hanged , stripped of my skin, I want that rather than not being with you.

57. Sweet Lord, I beseech you to make me die whatever death you want, as long as I am with you.

58. Oh, unhappy and weak that I am, I have waited for so long![2] Sweet Lord, why do you not break apart this miserable body so that I can be with you!

59. Sweet Lord, when will I see the hour when I am with you?

60. Sweetest Lord, when will you fulfill my desire?

61. Surely, lovely sweet Lord, I cannot find it in my heart that I want to be in this world any longer; but if it is your will that I stay longer I do not object for I know well that if I serve you longer, I will have more merit and a greater crown.[3]

62. Sweet Lord, you will be my crown for you are the crown of the virgins.

63. Sweet Lord, when I look at your holy incarnation and look at you in that small manger wrapped in poor rags, my heart is all on fire. And when I see you hanging on the cross, I want to be despised and disfigured for your love; and even more, I want to be able to die for your love and for the salvation of those that you so lovingly set free.

64. Oh, best Jesus Christ, what are your creatures doing? For I see hardly anyone who knows how to love or understand you; the religious behave and speak so irregularly that they are almost like secular people; and many are more eager to go to eat than to go to matins or mass.[4] They are very capable of drinking good wines and eating good food since they have it,[5] but they are incapable of remembering the smallest word told to them; on the contrary, by signs and words they return bad for bad.[6]

---

1 Lepers were outcasts in medieval society and often were obliged to walk around with a bell to warn people of their coming.

2 This sentence is not in Latin in the original text, but in Francoprovençal.

3 Lat. corona in the sense of the crown of martyrdom.

4 "Matins" is the first of the canonical hours, most commonly 3 a.m. The equivalences of the canonical hours and the times of day are not always fixed. See W. Rothwell, "The Hours of the Day in Medieval French," p. 241.

5 In the Latin, there is an amusing word play on "being capable" (potentes) and "of drinking" (potandum): "Ipsi sunt bene potentes ad potandum bona vina... ." (They are very capable of drinking good wines... .)

6 That is, do and say bad things to each other. The word "signs" refers to the habit in the Carthusian order to communicate not with words but with signs whenever possible.

65. Others seem to be so religious and so good since they like to go to church and restrain their passion so that do not dare raise their eyes, listen gladly to the word of God, fast, stay awake at night, and are full of great repentance, but they do not have the virtue of patience. Those are good, but not perfect. The friends of God must suffer persecution in this world, and truly they should not be impatient if someone does something evil to them; this should rather make them glad for they are finding something to sustain them in the love of their Lord. But others are so hardhearted, malicious, and haughty that—as soon as something is done or said to them that displeases them—they call out to God and curse those that did them harm.

66. Those who do this are not disciples of the Lord,[1] since He taught that we should not curse those who speak ill [of us]; on the contrary, He wants us to treat well those who do us harm.

67. When some think that they are close to the Lord, it seems to them that one should not say anything about them. Alas![2] A person may well believe to be close to the Lord when in reality he or she is far from Him; for Jesus Christ only lives in humble hearts and in those filled with peace, sweetness and charity.

68. A human being must have patience in tribulations and adversities and he or she must speak the truth because a mouth that lies kills the soul. And human beings must take care so that their hearts do not harbor improper thoughts, because Holy Scripture says that perverse thoughts separate [us] from God.[3]

69. Therefore everyone should take care to have within himself nothing but these virtues, and I truly believe that if he has these Jesus lives within him.

70. But what about those that only appear to be religious? They are so dissolute, so lazy in doing and saying good things, they are so sleepy during vigils and at all hours of the day when they should praise God that it is sickening to watch.

71. But when it comes to doing bad things, they are neither lazy nor sleepy. At night, when they should sleep and rest in order to

---

1 In Latin illi et ille, i.e., "those" in the masculine and the feminine. "Disciple," as well, appears in both the masculine and feminine forms in the Latin text.
2 As the exclamation in paragraph 58 (see p. 24, note 2) this phrase is in Francoprovençal and not in Latin. For her most emotional outbursts, Margaret resorts to her familiar everyday language.
3 See The Book of Wisdom 1:3 :"Perversae cogitationes separant a Deo" (Perverse thoughts separate [you] from God). The book of Wisdom is not a canonical book of the Bible, but it was part of the Vulgate version of the Bible current in the Middle Ages.

be able to praise God better and more devotedly, they begin to talk, to scold and tell lies.[1] It is impossible for a person who talks too much not to say a lot he or she should rather not say.

72. And there are people who do not know how to talk of anything that is good, but judge their brothers and sisters and, if they know of any fault in anyone, they rather talk about this than do something worthwhile.

73. And of people like these Saint Francis says that they are like the brothers of flies because the fly always lands in the worst place it can find on a human being; for wherever it finds a scab or a blemish, that is where it quickly settles. And for that reason those who cannot occupy themselves with anything worthwhile are called the brothers of flies.

74. Surely, everyone to whom God showed such grace in leading him away from the misery and dangers of this world, should feel great shame and confusion when he cannot direct his life towards fearing and loving God and his time towards serving Him, and when he cannot hold his tongue at the right time and place, and especially at bedtime, because many evils for both body and soul arise from this. Because of this, the body is not refreshed and and the soul loses God's devotion and grace, which is even more serious.

75. Alas! What great damage![2] How can one dismiss the great usefulness provided by the holy meditations which one should do during vigils; for man should meditate on the holy incarnation of Jesus Christ through which He wanted to become our brother, because of the great love He had for us; and through which He wanted to be born poor and be nailed naked to the cross and die a vile death. And through which He was resurrected from death to life and then rose to heaven to the right side of His glorious Father so that He could prepare the place and the reward for His friends.

76. Then one should meditate on the judgement of those who have to be judged and of which every single one who will get [what he deserves] according to his good or bad deeds. And surely one should take great care to be well prepared for death, since the hour of our death in uncertain. And for this reason it would be good to act according to the teachings and words of Solomon who says: that man who always thinks of the hour of his death will never sin.

77. Oh, Lord God, what shall those men and women do who go to hell running more quickly than a race horse? Any eagle flies with

---

1   Here we undoubtedly hear the voice of Margaret as prioress of a convent where she was in charge of daily discipline!

2   Again, this exclamation is in Francoprovençal.

a speed like that with which those people go to hell, and you should have no pity for them! Sweet Lord, you hid your bright face from them because of their sins and for that reason they are blind and do not know the bad things they pass through.

78. Oh, sweet lovely Lord, what shall they do if you do not have pity on them as long as they are still alive?

79. Sweet Lord, what shall they do on the day of judgment when they hear this terrible voice which will scream: "Rise you dead people, come to the judgment." Then the miserable will scream and tell the mountains and rocks to fall on them and hide them so that they do not have to face the judge[1]; but it will do them no good for they will have to come before him, whether they want to or not.

80. Alas! what shall the miserable sinners do and how shall they have to hold back since they won't dare to look at the world in front of them which will be consumed by fire and flames.

81. They will not dare to look to the right, for there will be accusing them all the evil deeds they have done since their birth. And all of them who will be there, good and evil, will see and recognize all their sins and will know who these people are who committed them.

82. They will not dare to look to their left, for there will be the devils who only wait for the judge to pronounce His sentence so that the sinners will fall into the pit of hell.

83. They will not dare to look down, for there they will see the pit of hell which has been prepared to receive them.

84. Then their conscience will be busy tormenting them and that will be one of the greatest tortures they will have to suffer.

85. Alas! How will they dare to look up when they will see the highest judge who will be furious for then He will be without any pity or compassion? Nor will His sweet mother then listen to one praying for the sinners, nor will the saints; but they will be so disturbed that the angels will cry bitterly, as the Holy Scripture says.

86. Then He will put the good on His right side, and the evil on His left.

87. Then He will say to those on his right side: "I was hungry and you gave me food; I was thirsty and you gave me drink; I was

---

1 Compare Rev. 6:16 where Saint John speaks of the Last Judgment: "They said to the mountains and the rocks: 'Fall on us and hide us away from the One who sits on the throne and from the anger of the Lamb.'"

a stranger and you welcomed me; I was naked and you clothed me; I was in prison and you visited me."[1]

88. To those on His left He will say reproachfully: "I was hungry and you gave me no food; I was thirsty and you gave me no drink; I was a stranger and you did not want to welcome me; I was naked and you did not clothe me; I was sick and in prison and you did not visit me."[2]

89. Alas! Who can think about this sentence that God pronounces on the evil and not have his heart break with the pain and pity for those who are in a state of sin; or when he realizes that they come to that painful moment when the highest judge tells them: "You cursed people, go into the hell fire which has been prepared for you, go with the devils who are waiting for you with their angels."[3]

90. After God will have pronounced this sentence the devils will hold ready their hooks with which they will pull those [sinners] down into the pit of hell. There will be burning flames, stinking sulphur, and devils in the form of snakes who will gnaw at the breasts and hearts of those who did not have true faith. There will be poisonous dragons who will eat the lips and tongues who blasphemed the name of the Lord Jesus Christ.[4]

91. Tortures fall on them as densely as the rain falls from the sky. Their bed cloths and covers will be of red coals and burning flames; the cauldron in which they will be trapped will be surrounded by horrible demons who will torment them as long as God lasts, in other words, until the end. Their food will be tears, pain, sighs, and gnashing of teeth. The cymbals and lutes they will hear will be noisy tempests and penetrating rivers which will pierce them through their hearts. They will have tunics and cloaks made of black pitch and resin which will stick to their bodies and, when their servants want to help them out of these [garments], they will undress them so cruelly that they will pull off not only the skin but also the flesh in several pieces down to the bone.

92. Then they will make them pass from one torture to another. They will suffer such hunger that they will eat their tongues and hands in anguish. They will suffer such thirst that their tongues

---

1 Paragraph 87 is almost a direct quotation of Matthew 25:35. Margaret omits the sentence "I was sick and you visited me."

2 See Matthew 25:42-43.

3 As I indicated in the Introduction, medieval people believed that as God has His angels as attendants, so does the devil.

4 For some medieval ideas on hell, see the Introduction, pp. 11-12.

will dry out and they will desire one drop of water every single day of their endless lives, and they will not get it.

93. They will hate each other so much that they would gladly gobble each other up if they could.

94. They will be without any hope of ever again having any compassion. Then they will scream like wild beasts, and I believe that this will be one of their greatest pains since they will be separated from the company of the glorified.

95. They will be in such darkness that they will never again see any light, but they will always see the devils before them ready to terrify and torment them.

96. Then the bodies will receive the retribution for the honors they had in the world; for they received their reward in this world and thus they will be tormented without end.

97. When God will have thus punished all evil people and will have separated from them forever, then He will renew the whole world, and the moon will shine as brightly as the sun, and the sun seven times as brightly as before.

98. Oh, sweet Lord God, who can imagine the great joy that the saints will have when you transfer the body of every single one of them, glorified and shining as the sun.

99. Then you will enter your glorious kingdom and you will call your friends by saying: "Come, O blessed of my Father, receive the glory that has been prepared for you from the beginning of the world,[1] enter into the joy and delights of your Lord." Then the queen of paradise and all saints will enter into the holy city of Jerusalem, praising and glorifying the Lord.

100. Because of this, lovely sweet Lord, when I think of the special graces you gave me in your solicitousness, [I remember] first, how you guarded me from infancy, and how you removed me from the perils of this world and called me to your holy service, and how you provided me with everything necessary to eat, to drink, to clothe and warm myself, so much so, that because of your great compassion I never had to worry about any of this.

101. Sweet Lord, when I was blind to my defects you quickly revealed them to me through your grace; when I was distressed you gave me your sweet comfort; and as you were doing all this, you gave me such honor and such grace that I do not know how to speak of it or to relate it, for I am not worthy. And yet I cannot keep from thinking of you, but still I think of you not as much as I should.

---

1   Compare Matthew 25:34.

Sweet Lord, I am stunned that my soul does not separate from the body when I think such things.

102. Sweet Lord, if you gave me no other grace than that you won't permit me to serve and be subject to men, I would be satisfied. And surely, sweet Lord, even if you did nothing else for me, I should well be drawn to loving you; for you never gave me a grace—except for your Passion—for which I am so deeply grateful and which draws my heart as strongly towards loving you as that: that you wanted me and let me be joined to no one but you.

103. Oh, sweet lovely Lord Jesus Christ, how did I pay you back until today for all the good you did to me? Surely, my sweet Lord, I paid you with nothing but villainy and outrage. Sweet Lord, I paid you back with evil for the good you did to me.

104. My sweet Lord, I offer you my gratefulness for your compassion, for you did not permit me to die with my sins.

105. My sweet Lord, truly, when I take a good look at the grace and good things you gave me amd at the great rewards you promise those that serve you, my mind is completely transformed and I lose all desire to offend you.

106. And from now on I want to direct my whole life towards loving you and my time towards serving you, and for the times past, sweet Lord, when I was so deficient because of my sins and my negligence, I beg you for your pity and true indulgence. And I pray and beseech you for your sweetness and great compassion to give me perfect humility so that I can nurture and guard within me the fire of your holy love, without extinguishing it, just like the fire of live coals. And I beg you to choose me for your glorious realm and to remove from me everything that could displease you. And I beg you to give me the grace of the Holy Spirit to enlighten me and to teach me to do worthwhile acts of penance.

107. Sweet Lord, I beg you to help me since my enemies surround me: the world, the flesh, the devil. The world invites me with its honors and its riches to find my pleasure there. The flesh is full of laziness and sleepiness and always goes against the spirit. The devil labors day and night to entrap me and make me sin. But I trust in your great goodness, for just as I have put beneath my feet the world which I do not value any more than something completely worthless,[1] I truly believe that you will make me vanquish the flesh and the devil with all his insults.

---

1 The exact translation would be "than something hanging from a fork." Margaret uses a number of homely similes, such as her reference to wool rags in paragraph 26.

108. My sweet dear Lord, truly when I meditate well on the pain and anguish which I suffered through my love in this world, everything that used to please me and delight me I now hate, and everything that used to be unpleasant and hard for me to bear is now sweetness and consolation, and I [now] love that which I used to despise as much as that which I consider valuable.

109. Sweet Lord, write into my heart what you want me to do. Write your law, write there your orders so that they will never be erased.

110. Sweet Lord, I know well that my flesh is full of laziness and sleepiness, but my spirit is ready to do your will.

111. Sweet Lord, I used to reject your consolation, but now when I remember you, I delight in desire and love for you, sweet Lord.

112. Here end the holy meditations of the sacred virgin Margaret, prioress of the convent of Poleteins, of the Carthusian Order.

Mirror

Chapter 1[1]

1. It seems to me that you have heard it said that, when you listen to someone tell of some grace given by our Lord to some of His friends, you are the better for it for a long time. And because I desire your salvation as my own, I will tell you, as briefly as possible, of a great favor done not long ago to a person of my acquaintance.[2] And so that you will profit from this as much as possible, I will tell you the reason why God, in my opinion, did this favor for her.

2. By the grace of our Lord, this creature had written into her heart the holy life that Jesus Christ had led on earth, His good examples and His good teachings. She had put sweet Jesus Christ

---

1 *Speculum* (or *Mirror*) was a title frequently given to didactic treatises, both spiritual and historical (e.g. the thirteenth- century *Speculum historiale*, or "historical mirror" of Vincent of Beauvais). There is a note in the manuscript which explains that in the year 1294, Hugo, prior of Vallebonne, brought the *Mirror* to the prior of the Charterhouse. The account of the vision, i.e. the *Mirror*, had been given to him by "the servant of God, lady Margaret, prioress from Poleteins. And it is believed that this vision was written by this prioress to whom God gave such grace that He deigned to reveal such secrets to her."

2 See the Introduction for the use of the third person to tell about first-person visionary experiences.

so firmly into her heart that it sometimes seemed to her that He was present and that He held a closed book in His hand in order to teach from it.

3. The outside of this book was completely covered with white, black and red letters; the clasps of the book had golden letters on them.[1]

4. In the white letters was written the saintly life of the blessed Son of God who was all white through His great innocence and His holy works. In the black letters were written the blows and the slaps and the filthy things that the Jews had thrown at His saintly face and His noble body until He looked like a leper. In the red letters were written the wounds and the precious blood that was shed for us.

5. There were also two clasps that closed the book; they had gold letters on them. On one of them was written: "God will be everything to everyone." On the other one was written: "God is marvelous in His saints."[2]

6. Now I will tell you briefly how this creature studied this book. When morning came she began to think of the manner in which the blessed Son of God wanted to descend to the misery of this world, take on our humanity and join it to His divinity, so that one can say that God, who was immortal, died for us. Then she thought of the great humility that was in Him. Then she thought about how He always wanted to be persecuted. Then she thought of His great poverty and His great patience and how He was obedient until death.

7. After she had looked into this book carefully, she began to read in the book of her conscience which she found full of falsity and lies. When she considered the humility of Jesus Christ, she found herself full of pride. When she thought of how He wanted to be scorned and persecuted, she found in herself just the opposite. When she considered His poverty, she did not find it in her that

---

1 This book recalls the book described in Rev. 5:1: "And I saw in the right hand of him who was seated on the throne a scroll written within and on the back, sealed with seven seals." The colors, aside from their symbolic value, are among those used in medieval book writing and illumination. As for their symbolism, there are other texts of that period which assign similar functions to these colors. Why does Margaret say "written in the letters"? It could be that she thought she saw large initials which, in medieval books, often contained complex images.

2 The first quote is from 1. Corinthians 15:28, the second from Psalm 67:36 (68:35): "*Mirabilis est Deus in sanctis suis.*" The correct translation is "Terrible is God in His sanctuary." ("Sanctis" means in the sanctuary or holy place.) But since Margaret herself gives a different translation of this quote in paragraph 22, I translate it here as she does later.

she wanted to be so poor that she would be scorned. When she considered His patience, she found none in herself. When she thought of the way in which He was patient until death, she did not find herself as obedient as she should have been.

8. These were the white letters in which the life of the blessed Son of God had been written. Then, when she had well considered all her faults she made an effort to correct them, as much as she could, following the example of the life of Jesus Christ.

9. Then she studied the black letters, in which were written the evil things which had been done to Jesus Christ: in these letters she learned to bear tribulations with patience.

10. Then she studied the red letters, in which were written the wounds of Jesus Christ and the shedding of His precious blood. In these letters she not only learned to bear tribulations with patience, but also to enjoy them, so that all the pleasures of this world became detestable to her; and to such an extent that it seemed to her that there was nothing in this world as worthy and as sweet as suffering the pains and the torments of this worlds for the love of her creator.

11. Then she studied the gold letters. There she learned to desire the things of heaven.

12. In this book she found written the life that Jesus Christ led on earth, from His birth until the time when he went up to heaven.

13. Then she began to think about how the blessed Son of God is sitting on the right side of His glorious father. But her fleshly eyes[1] were still so darkened that she could not contemplate our Lord in heaven. But she always had to return to the beginning of the life that our Lord Jesus Christ led on earth, until she had amended her life, based on the example of this book. In this way, she meditated for a long time

Chapter 2

14. Not long ago, she was praying after matins, and she began to look at her book, as was her habit. When she was not expecting it, it seemed to her that the book opened itself: until then, she had only seen it from the outside.

15. The inside of this book was like a beautiful mirror, and there were only two pages. Of the things she saw in this book I will tell you only little, for I have neither the understanding that could conceive of it, nor the mouth that could tell it. Nevertheless, I will tell you some of it, if God gives me the grace to do it.

---

1   As opposed to her "spiritual eyes."

16. In this book appeared a delightful place, so large that the entire world seems small by comparison. In this place appeared a glorious light which divided itself into three parts, like three persons, but there is no human mouth that could speak of it.

17. From this place came all possible good things. From there came the true wisdom through which all things are made and created. There was the power whose will everything obeys. From there came such great sweetness and such great comfort that the angels and the souls were so satisfied by it that they could desire nothing else. From there came such a good odor that it drew to itself all the virtues of heaven. From there came such a great glow of love that all the loves of this world are only great bitterness compared to this love. From there came a joy so great that no human heart could imagine it.

18. When the angels and the saints contemplate the great beauty of Our Lord and feel His goodness and His great sweetness, they feel such great joy that they cannot keep from singing; but they sing a song which is all new and of such sweetness that it is a wonderful melody.[1] This sweet song makes its way through all the orders of the angels and the saints, from the first to the last. And this song is hardly finished when they start another one, also all new. And this song will last forever.

19. The saints will be within their Creator as the fish within the sea: they will drink as much as they want, without getting tired and without diminishing the amount of water. The saints will be just like that, for they will drink and eat the great sweetness of God. And the more they will get, the greater their hunger will be. This sweetness cannot decrease any more or less than can the water of the sea. For just as the rivers all come out of the sea and go back to it, so it is for the beauty and sweetness of Our Lord: although they flow everywhere, they always return to Him. And for that reason they can never grow smaller.

20. Even if the saints did nothing but think of His great goodness, they could never completely imagine the great charity in virtue of which the good Lord sent His blessed son to earth.

21. Now think that in Him there are also other goods. He is all one can imagine or desire in all the saints. And this is the inscrip-

---

1 "A new song"—often signifying Christ—is a term used in the book of Revelation 5:9: "And they sung a new song saying, Thou art worthy to take the book, and to open the seals thereof." This is one of the many echoes of the book of Revelation we find in the *Mirror*. It links the book of Margaret's vision to the book with seven seals.

tion that was written on the first clasp of the book: "God will be everything to everyone."

22. On the second clasp was written: *"Mirabilis Deus in sanctis suis*, God is marvelous in His saints."[1] There is no human intelligence that could imagine how marvellous God is in His saints.

Chapter 3

23. Not long ago a person of my acquaintance was praying around matins and began to think of Jesus Christ, how He is seated to the right of God the Father. And right away her heart was so ravished that she thought she was in a place much larger than the entire world, and more brilliant all over than the sun; and it was full of such beautiful and glorious people that no human mouth could tell of it.

24. Among others, she seemed to see Jesus Christ, so glorious that no human heart could conceive of it. He was clothed in this glorious garment which He assumed in the noble body of Our Lady. On His noble hands and feet appeared the glorious wounds that He suffered for love of us. From these glorious wounds poured forth such a great light that one was stunned by it: it was as if all the beauty of the Divinity was passed on through it. This glorious body was so noble and so transparent that one could clearly see the soul inside of it. This body was so noble that one could see oneself reflected in it, more clearly than in a mirror. This body was so beautiful that one could see the angels and the saints, as if they were painted on it. His face was so graceful that the angels who had looked upon it from the moment of their creation could not get enough of it but always desired to look at Him.

25. Surely, if one conceived of and considered the beauty and goodness that is within Him, one would love Him so much that all other things would appear to be bitter. For He is so good and so sweet and so courteous that He has shared with His friends all that is good.

26. Now imagine His great beauty, so great that He has given to all the angels and all the saints who are His members, the gift of being as brilliant as the sun. You can imagine how beautiful the place is where there are so many brilliant lights.

27. For God is so great that He is everywhere, and no one is capable of this but He. He gave to his friends such lightness that in one instant they can go wherever they want; in fact, wherever they are, they are in His presence.

---

1   On this quote see p. 42, note 2.

28. God is very strong and very powerful, and because of that He has given to His friends such power and such strength that they can do whatever they want: if they had the desire to lift the entire world with their little finger, they could do it easily.

29. Jesus Christ is totally free, and because of that He has made His friends so free, subtle and immaterial that they can enter and leave, through closed doors, without any hindrance, as Jesus Christ did after the resurrection.

30. God cannot suffer and cannot have any sickness within Him, and because of that He has given to His friends such good health that they can never be sick, nor depressed, nor suffering, neither in soul nor in body.

31. God is the highest joy, and there is no delight nor true joy that does not come from Him. He is the sweet electuary in which are all good flavors. He is so good that those who taste Him will be all the more hungry the more they receive, and they will not dare to desire anything but the sweetness they feel from Him.[1]

32. God is full of wisdom, and He has given so much of it to His friends that they will never have to ask for anything, for they will have everything they desire.

33. God is love, and He has given so much of it to the saints that they love each other as one member loves another. And what one of them wants, the others want too.

34. God is eternal, and because of that He has made His friends of such noble matter that they cannot become ugly nor age, but they will live with Him forever.

35. Now you can imagine the great goodness that is in Him who has thus given everything He has to His friends. He did even more for them, for He has given Himself. He made them so beautiful and so glorious that each of them sees the Trinity in himself, as one sees in a beautiful mirror that which is in front of it. And this is the inscription that was on the second clasp, where it was written: *"Mirabilis Deus in sanctis suis."*[2]

36. And just as the saints take pleasure in seeing the beauty of Our Lord, so our good Creator takes pleasure in the beauty and love of the beautiful creatures He has made in His image and semblance: thus a good master likes to look at a beautiful painting when he has painted it well.

37. I truly believe that he who would devote his heart to the contemplation of the great beauty of Our Lord and of the glory that

---

1   For ideas related to God or Christ as food see Bynum, *Holy Feast and Holy Fast*.

2   See p. 42, note 2.

He manifests in His saints, he could rightly say that these are true marvels, and I believe he would fall into a swoon; he could say that God kept the promise He made to His saints through the prophet David: "I say, you are gods."[1] For it seems to everyone one of them that he is a little god, because they will be His sons and heirs.

38. I truly believe that there is not a heart in this world so cold that it would not be set on fire with love, if it could imagine and know the very great beauty of Our Lord. But there are some hearts so debased that they are like the pig who prefers the smell of the mire to that of a beautiful rose. Those who prefer to think about the things of this world and find more comfort there than in God are like that.[2] And those people are so full of darkness that they see nothing.

39. And people who are so impure do not have the power to love God nor to know Him. For God says in the gospel that no one knows the Son except the Father, and no one the Father except the Son and those to whom the Son wishes to reveal Him. I truly believe that the Son of God does not reveal His secrets to people who are impure, and that is why the pure of heart are blessed, because they will see God clearly.[3] He Himself promises this in the gospel and He says that blessed are the pure of heart, for they will see God face to face in His great beauty.[4]

40. May Jesus Christ grant us to live in such great purity of heart and body that, when our souls leave our bodies, He will deign to show us His glorious face. Amen.

Here ends the Mirror of the holy virgin Margaret, prioress of Poleteins; she died in the year of Our Lord 1310, on February 11.

The Life of the Virgin Saint Beatrice of Ornacieux
Chapter 1[5]

41. In honor of God and in praise of His blessed name, in order to recognize his great compassion, and to give Him thanks for the

---

1 Psalm 81:6(82:6): "Ego dixi: Dii estis…" (I have said: You are gods).

2 That is, like the pig.

3 The Francoprovençal word is "apertement," a word frequently used in medieval texts to describe things that will be revealed.

4 This phrase recalls the well-known verse from 1. Corinthians 13:12: "For now we see in a mirror dimly, but then face to face." The King James version is more dramatic: "For now we see in a glass, darkly…."

5 Although Beatrice of Ornacieux is called a saint here, she has, at the present time, not yet reached this distinction: so far she has only been beatified.

glorious gifts of his goodness, in order to be more fervent in the service of our Lord Jesus Christ and of his glorious virgin mother, I want humbly and piously to write a part of the of the pure, saintly and wise life which this spouse of Jesus Christ led on earth, among her sisters, from the age of thirteen on.[1]

42. We know that at the beginning of her saintly life she voluntarily and honestly resolved to escape from all things of this world for the love of Jesus Christ. She kept this good resolution very faithfully.

43. She was very humble in her thoughts and actions. She was very charitable and compassionate and cared for her companions in all humility. She inflicted on herself fasts and abstinences which were as severe as her feeble constitution could bear. She was wholly obedient and eager at prayer; she had such ardent devotion that, several times, she thought she would lose her eye-sight because of the many tears she shed.[2] She was also very kind in everything she said; she was humble and a great example to everyone.

44. She was very zealous and fervent in applying all her intelligence to doing, seeing and understanding everything that seemed useful to her for the edification of her own soul and that of other people. We know that in the course of this saintly life our Lord, in His great compassion, bestowed many graces on her.

45. In the beginning and for a long time, every day, whatever she was doing and wherever she was, grace was so plentiful that it seemed to her that our lord was always manifestly at her side. Then our Lord increased His grace to such a degree that she felt—no matter where she was—such great grace and such a radiance of the Lord's love in her heart that she could hardly bear it. In this manifestation of grace He came to her like a person who kissed her vigorously and lovingly. In that sweetness which she felt through the sweet kisses of her true Creator, it seemed to her that she would faint.[3]

1   See Weinstein and Bell *Saints and Society* chs. 1 and 2 on the age when holiness became manifest. Girls as young as four or five were sometimes given to a convent. In the Carthusian order one knows of eleven and twelve-year old nuns.
2   See the Introduction for tears as a sign of holiness.
3   Fainting for the love of Christ was a typical expression of a mystical experience.

46. After she had led this saintly life for a long time, the devil began to direct all his efforts towards tormenting her in all possible ways. And when she saw that he planned to deceive her in such an ugly way, she began to impose a great penance on herself. Because she was so afraid of the deceptions of the devil she used practices in this penance which were sometimes immoderate.[1] But she did everything in great fear [of God] and with great fervor; and every time, our Lord put everything back in order.[2]

47. When she was a cook and a nurse, she showed great charity.[3] And when she had to do something on the fire, she moved her face so close to the heat that it seemed to her that her brain was on fire and that her eyes came out of her head, and often she expected to see them falling on the floor.

48. She always carried live coals in her naked hands so that her skin burned completely, including her palms. Of all this, she felt nothing.

49. She punished herself so severely that blood was running down her body on all sides.[4]

50. She evoked the Passion of our Lord so strongly that she pierced her hands with blunt nails until it came out at the back of her hand. And every time she did this, clear water without any blood in it gushed out. Soon after, the wound closed and healed so well that nobody could see it any more.[5]

51. When she could not do anything else, she walked through the snow and ice without shoes.

52. When the devil saw that she mortified herself so greatly and that he could achieve nothing as long as she was awake, he began

1 This lack of moderation, absent from Margaret's own life, characterized many mystics.
2 It is not quite clear what Margaret refers to here. Maybe she means that Beatrice was restored physically; or she may refer to the Lord's preventing further excesses of penance.
3 In most convents, the nuns took turns in doing the jobs necessary for the daily life of the sisters.
4 The Francoprovençal word is *discipline* which can mean discipline or punishment but which can also refer to the whips used in acts of penance (most dramatically and publicly by the flagellants, a group of penitents in the thirteenth and fourteenth centuries, who would roam the streets calling on the sinners to beg in this way for God's forgiveness!).
5 For an interesting treatment of experiences involving fire and "holy marks" in contemporary fiction, see Louise Erdrich, *Love Medicine* (1984; Bantam Books 1987), ch. 2, "Saint Marie." After a nun named Leopolda has stabbed the heroine with a fork, she covers up her deed by saying: "I have told my Sisters of your passion... How the stigmata... the mark of nails... appeared in your palm and you swooned at the holy vision" (p. 55). (The reenactment of Jesus' being nailed to the cross is called stigmatization. It was a common experience among saints [see for example Saint Francis] but did not always involve actual nails. Often the stigmata were sent miraculously from heaven.)

to torment her in her sleep much more than he had done when she was awake.

53. He omitted none of the things that could do harm to her soul or body and displease her Creator, and he offered them to her in her imagination and through images as nastily as he could. Nobody would dare describe the horrible foulness and filth which he paraded before her eyes in various ways, but she knew nothing of all this and nothing could harm her.

54. When he had done this several times and had tried everything and saw that he would not get anywhere, he made as if he was hurling arrows at her. Then it seemed to her that these arrows, which were made from manifold and filthy sins, hit her soul from all sides, but they could not harm her.

Chapter 2

55. When she saw that this would not end but was getting worse all the time, she began to be more and more afraid.

56. One night when she was in her bed she was in such great terror that she began to implore Our Lady to help and rescue her and in her great pity to protect her from the power and tricks of the devil.

57. When she had said her prayer Our Lady came to her and it seemed to her that Our Lady was fifteen years old and of such beauty that it was impossible to describe. Then the glorious Lady turned lovingly towards her with a look filled with pity and sweetness and said to her: "Dearest daughter, do not fear anything," she said, "I am the mother of the all powerful king whose spouse you are,[1] and I am the mother of compassion, and by virtue of this power and compassion I take your soul and your body under my guard and protection and I will protect and defend you against the power of the devil and his tricks."

58. The she left her. And immediately the devil left her in peace and she enjoyed complete peace.

59. Another night, not much later, he appeared before her with the intention of deceiving and violently tormenting her in another way; but as soon as she began to invoke Our Lady and to recite "Ave Maria" Our Lady rescued her, and he departed, all confused. And he disappeared into the earth in the shape of a large black cloud of smoke. And when he disappeared into the earth, the earth shook violently at the place where he disappeared.

---

1 For the nun as a bride of Christ see the Introduction.

60. From that moment on she received even more grace from our Lord.

61. A long time after all these events and after our Lord had given her many other proofs of his grace and secret revelations, she began to wish so ardently to be with our Lord that she began to ask our Lord for death, and she did this insistently.

Chapter 3

62. During that time it happened that one night after vespers she was praying before the altar, and on that day someone had by accident removed the container in which is kept the Body of our Lord[1] from the tabernacle and had put it in one of the niches in the altar. While praying she turned to that side and, crying profusely, begged our Lord for death. Then, during her prayer, she heard the voice of her Creator who spoke from the container which I mentioned above as standing in the niche.

63. We know that among other things people asked her what kind of voice and which words she believed to have heard. She answered that it was a male voice, as far as she could make out, but it was so different that she did not think that any man on earth could conceive of anything in his heart or express through his mouth anything that would resemble or could be compared to the great beauty and sweetness of that voice and of those glorious words.

64. While He was speaking to her, He told her clearly not to desire such a thing and not to ask Him for such a thing; "for," He said, "I do not want you to die yet". He told her that so kindly and so lovingly that she was convinced that neither she nor anyone else would ever be able to convey this impression. And the great desire of death that she had left her heart immediately and she was greatly comforted; now she desired to keep on living in the service of our Lord.

65. At that moment it came to her that the illness which had resulted from her weakness could be harmful to her serving our Lord and she immediately began to pray with great devotion.

66. Among other prayers she said the following: "Dearest Lord, my true God and good Creator, I beg of the profound mercy of your divinity and of the compassionate charity of your powerful humanity that it may please you—and because it is your will that I go on living—to give me health for my soul and my body and especially for the illness of my head, so that I may always have

---

1 That is, the Host (the holy wafer).

your grace and will always be able to persevere in your service with devotion, as long as it will please you in your goodness to keep me alive."

67. During that prayer she heard, as she had heard it before, the glorious voice of her true Creator who said to her: "Receive and bear in my name anything that I may send you." He said this to her very cheerfully and almost, it seemed to her, with a smile. The comfort that she had felt earlier had been so great that she would not have been able to express it; but afterwards it was even greater and the grace of our Lord was always within her.

Chapter 4

68. Another time it happened that a brother of hers was at war. The great compassion she felt for his being in captivity prompted her to pray to our Lord. Deeply distressed, she begged him to liberate her brother from the hands of his enemies. And she prayed so much that one day, as she was praying in church, she fell asleep and it seemed to her that she saw two people coming from heaven, and they were the most beautiful creatures of the world. They moved to the right side of the altar and it seemed to her that they straightened up [the floor around it] and wiped it clean.

69. When they had done this diligently, she saw two other people coming and they were incomparably more beautiful than the first two. Their heads were lowered; they seemed sorrowful. They began to display a very beautiful cloth made of gold.

70. Then she saw two more people approaching, and they were even more beautiful than the others. And those who were displaying the cloth gave them the end that was near the altar and they held it up high; then the others who held the cloth low spread it out on the floor which the first two had prepared so carefully; and then, with great respect, they put down the cloth.

71. When that was done, she saw a great crowd coming nearer and they were without comparison, more resplendent than the sun in its greatest brightness. And all of them, as they were approaching, bowed down in the direction of the altar, towards the side where the Body of our Lord was, and their lowered faces seemed to show great pity. The first and the last groups united and then they separated and formed two choirs.

72. Then she saw other people even more beautiful than the previous ones who joined the two choirs, and the choirs all bowed with great respect. This last group was so large that one could not count them and they formed two other choirs.

73. Between these two choirs which had joined the first two a person appeared who was held by four others; two held Him by the

head and two by the feet. It seemed to her that these four people were the noblest creatures of all. They put the glorious body that they had been holding on the gold cloth the others had prepared. When they put down this glorious body, the four choirs approached and knelt down respectfully before Him. And the four people held a cloth of gold on which there were thirteen precious stones, and every single one of them radiated such vivid brightness that it seemed to her that if the whole world had been plunged into complete darkness, it could have been completely illuminated through the tiniest spark that the smallest of these stones gave off.

74. She thought that this could only be the glorious body of the sweet Creator, the true Son of God. And she had wanted to be daring and address a little prayer to Him. But then she did not even dare to look in His direction.

75. Then she saw four people who separated themselves from the four choirs and came fearfully towards her. They knelt down and took the cloth that the others were holding above Him and pulled it down beyond His feet, so that His whole precious body appeared, stretched out on the cloth that was on the floor, and He held up His hands and feet. He elevated them so much that the wounds on His hands, His feet and His side appeared, as red and fresh as on the day and in the hour that they were made, and the crown also was visible on His head.[1]

76. Since she desired so greatly to address a small prayer to Him, He looked sweetly in her direction and, with great compassion, said to her: "Oh, my dearest daughter and spouse, come closer and do not fear anything, but look at your true Creator and know your Savior. And meditate carefully on what you will see of the terrible suffering and tortures that had to be borne by your good Creator, the true son of God, for your salvation and for the salvation of all humans; when you contemplate this truth, you will find more than you desire".

77. Then she answered: "Oh! My true God and my true Savior, without your grace I could not contemplate nor meditate profoundly on what you tell me".

78. Then He told her briefly: "I will give you understanding of all things at another time. But now you may ask from me whatever you want."

---

1 As the editors of Margaret's texts point out, this paragraph recalls the liturgy of Good Friday, in particular the devotion to the wounds of Christ. The stigmatization of Saint Francis, they note, had oriented religious thought toward these wounds (p. 162).

79. Then, very fearfully, she asked Him for several things that He granted her in His great goodness. Among other things, she asked Him that it may please His great mercy to liberate her brother from the hands of his enemies; and He granted her everything. And as soon as He had granted her this last grace, everything that she had seen vanished.

80. That same day she heard that her brother had been freed. And she carefully asked at what time he had been liberated and she found that it was the same moment in which the Lord had granted her her brother's freedom.

Chapter 5

81. It happened another time that she had gone to sleep after compline.[1] And soon, without her being asleep, it seemed to her that her spirit was among the saints of paradise; and it seemed to her that she saw so many of them that it would have been impossible to count them. As for their beauty, it seemed to her that the sun in its greatest and most beautiful radiance was nothing compared to the great beauty of the saints she saw next to her and on all sides and even above her in the air. But she saw them not physically, but spiritually;[2] and she saw her own body in the bed, and it looked like a dead body.

82. To our knowledge, she never wanted to reveal of this vision anything but the fact that she could neither describe nor understand it; and it was the same with the profound and secret revelations in which the Lord showed her the assembly of the glorious saints.

Chapter 6

83. For a long period of time every day at the elevation she saw the Body of our Lord un the form of a little child.[3] Thus she saw a great brightness between the priest's hands, so vivid and so bright

---

1 Compline (also called *completa*) is the last of the canonical hours of daily prayer around 9 p.m..

2 This is a common terminology in visionary experiences. Saint Jerome writes of his protegee Paula: "She cried out in my hearing that with the eyes of her soul she could see the infant Christ..." (Sumption, *Medieval Pilgrimage*, p. 91). Hildegard of Bingen introduces one of her visions as follows: "But I saw these visions not in dreams, nor sleeping, nor in frenzy, nor with the eyes of my body... but...with the eyes and ears of the interior man" (Preface of *Scivias*, transl. F.M. Steele, in Petroff, p. 151).

3 The elevation of the host is the moment in the ritual of the mass when, according to Catholic doctrine, the holy wafer is transformed into the actual flesh of the Lord. The vision of an infant in the host is not uncommon in medieval spirituality, as we saw in the Introduction.

and of such wonderful beauty that in her opinion it could not be compared to anything the human spirit could imagine.

84. It seemed to her that this brightness had a circular shape and that in the brightness there appeared a great red brightness, so resplendent and so beautiful that it illuminated with its great beauty all of the white brightness.

85. And in that white brightness appeared a little child; she could not describe nor make anyone understand the great beauty of this child. Above this child there appeared a great brightness which looked like gold; it gave off such a vivid brilliance that it enfolded all the other brightnesses into itself and entered itself into the other brightnesses. And the other brightnesses enfolded that last one, while they themselves entered into it.[1] These four visions manifested themselves in the same manner and with the same beauty and splendor. And it seemed to her that the beauty and splendor they had in common appeared united in that child. And that child appeared in the midst of this splendor.

86. After she had enjoyed this vision for a long time, she thought she was a great sinner and that she was offending her Creator, and she began to be fearful. So she anxiously begged of our Lord that it may please His great goodness to show her His glorious body quite simply at elevation. After that prayer she saw him for some time as one can see from afar an image painted on parchment.[2] Nevertheless His beauty was so great that she could not describe nor make anyone understand it. After that, she saw Him quite simply, as the other nuns did.

Chapter 7

Another time, during Advent,[3] her heart was greatly troubled: it seemed to her that our Lord had forgotten her because in her prayers she had no longer her habitual fervor and devotion. And therefore, as Christmas approached her pain increased. On Christmas Day, before mass, on Christmas Eve and the day before that, she made a great effort to confess everything that she had ever thought, done or said that could have displeased our Lord.

---

1   This complicated pattern of the three (white, red and gold) brightnesses with the child in the middle seems to be a representation of the Trinity which is three (Father, Son and Holy Ghost), yet one.

2   In the Middle Ages books were made from folios of parchment (stretched animal skin). Often they were illuminated, that is, decorated with beautiful initials or full-scale miniatures. Margaret refers to the latter here.

3   Advent is the month before Christmas. The four Sundays preceding Christmas are called "First, Second, Third and Fourth Advent."

Still, this did not seem to be enough for her to dare to go to communion.

89. When her companions began to approach the altar for communion, she stayed behind with so many tears and such a grievous pain that she thought her soul would leave her body. In that great pain she reflected that all her companions received their Savior,[1] while she—on that day when He had consented to being born into this world for our salvation—did not dare take communion because of the great sins she believed to have committed. Then she thought she would have to have recourse to the great mercy of her sweet Creator.

90. And she begged Him to instruct her so that she would learn what He wanted: should she receive [the Host] or abstain?

91. At that moment she felt such a great desire to receive her Creator that she almost fainted before she even got to the altar.

92. When she had received the blessed body of our Lord and was returning to her seat, she felt that a lentil-sized piece of the Hosthad remained in her mouth. And right away she felt a kind of bitterness in her heart which frightenend her greatly, and she did all she could to swallow what was left in her mouth, but she could not do it.

93. When she was back at her seat, she cried so hard that she could not see anything any more, and the Hostthat she still had in her mouth began to grow until her mouth was completely filled by it. And she was so troubled by the feeling of her mouth being so full that she put her hand to her mouth and almost pulled the Hostout of it. But some unknown force held it back, and she tasted flesh and blood. No one would dare to tell of her great fear when this happened.

94. Among other prayers which she addressed to our Lord in her heart she asked that, through His mercy, He put an end to her life in this very hour; or else that He give her some advice and consolation in her great fear.

95. While she was praying so devotedly that she fainted, she swallowed what she had in her mouth without noticing it until the moment when she felt it penetrate her heart. She felt such great joy and comfort in her heart that she thought she would faint completely.

96. She remained thus comforted until mass and the noon office were all finished. Between noon and the moment when the convent went to eat she saw and learned many secrets of our Lord that she

---

1 That is, the Host.

never wanted to talk about. Still, we know that she had entered such a profound contemplation that she could justly recite the verse which says: "As we have heard in the city of the Lord."[1]

97. After that, she regained physical consciousness and saw that she was not at table with the others in the community; she thought that the prioress and the others would be astonished that on such a day she was not a part of the community because she had not asked permission to go to table; so right away she asked for permission to go to table. She wanted to force herself to eat so as not to astonish the others, but she couldn't, however much she tried, and she had to remove from her mouth a small piece of bread that she had taken and which for her had no more taste than earth. And from the moment when she had said grace with the community until the hour when nones was rung,[2] she remained in such profound contemplation that our good Creator once more revealed to her many secrets, and He did so in a vision so sweet and delightful that she could well say like Saint Paul in his letter: "What no eye has seen, nor [ear] heard etc."[3]

98. During the three days of Christmas she felt this great consolation all the time, except that she had the vision only on the first day; but the great consolation and love of her good Creator were so abundant in her heart that she could no longer eat or sleep. The fourth day of Christmas she felt some displeasure in her heart and immediately the feeling of consolation left her—but not completely—and she returned to her former state which was good before [the vision] and was even better afterwards.

Chapter 8

99. After all these graces and some others given to her by our good Creator, she remained for two years without receiving any special grace from our Lord; but she kept up her good works and seemed to feel more and more fear and love of God.

100. At the end of these two years, there was not a single day, from the feast day of Saint Anthony to the second week of Lent,[4] that night or day she did not see or learn about some of the secrets of our Lord. These secrets were so great and marvellous that whenever she thought she could tell about a part of these

---

1 This incomplete quote from Psalm 47:9 (48:8) is in Latin in the Francoprovençal text: "Sicut audivimus, [sic vidimus,] in civitate Domini."
2 Nones is the ninth canonical hour or about 3 p.m.
3 In Latin in the text: "Quod oculus non vidit nec [*auris*] audivit et cetera" (I Corinthians 2:9). The word auris is missing in Margaret's quote.
4 The feast day of Saint Anthony is January 17. Lent is the forty-day period of fasting between Ash Wednesday and Easter.

secrets, [her listener] could never retain anything because God would not permit it: perhaps the person to whom she wanted to reveal the secrets was not worthy of remembering them.

101. Still, we know that she saw the coming of our Lord and His Passion and His Resurrection and His Ascension and how He was received at the right of His glorious Father. In these visions she saw such important, such secret and such hard to understand things that, as far as we know, no one can understand them, neither through intelligence nor through learning, unless the Holy Spirit opens a person's eyes of the heart.[1]

102. In these visions was revealed to her the significance of the twelve stones[2] on the gold cloth with which He was covered, as we told above. And the significance of what He said to her was also revealed: that she should look upon her true Creator and should know her true Savior and that she should meditate carefully—according to that which she would see—on the great height, the great depth and breadth of the terrible sufferings and many torments borne by our good Creator. And it was explained to her what He said: that in the meditation on this truth she would find more than she could ever desire.

103. During this time, from the feast day of Saint Anthony until the second week of Lent, every day, as soon as she had gone to sleep after complines, she entered into this secret vision which was shown to her in various ways.

104. She remained in this vision from the moment she had gone to sleep after complines until a little before noon the next day. Still, we do not know whether she had a full vision of the eternal glory, except during one hour at night. Besides that, as soon as day and matins drew near, because of the vision and the great secrets of her good Creator, she experienced such great consolation and joy that she had hardly any consciousness of her body and she it seemed to her that she was fainting and she had the impression that she was only spirit.

105. The day after these revelations of joy and eternal glory she experienced another kind of vision and revelation, full of such great pain and terror that one could never tell about it. [It was so horrible] that during this vision she almost forgot the great joy and the great glory she had seen the night before, and she thought she would sink into despair. But the little that she managed to recall

1 The "eyes of the heart" denote a different type of understanding: not intellectual, but rather emotional and unmediated by reason.
2 The stones were mentioned in paragraph 73, except that there Margaret spoke of thirteen stones.

of the vision and the glory of her good Creator and also of His mercy kept up her faith and hope.

106. In this horrible vision she saw the terrible and frightful pains suffered by the sinners for different kinds of sins; and the great variety of terrible pains corresponded to the variety of grievous sins.

107. Among other things she saw how the wrath of God descended on the sinners, and then she saw how God in His Incarnation transformed His wrath into pity and mercy. She saw how Our Lady reminded her glorious Son how she had carried Him in her glorious body, and how she had given birth to Him, nourished and suckled Him for the deliverance and the salvation of the sinners; and she saw how our Lord reminded His glorious Father of the death and the passion and the wounds and the nails and the lance and the crown and the spilling of His precious blood and the other sufferings and the various torments He bore in His humanity in order to save the human race.[1] She saw how Our Lady succeeded in appeasing our good Creator with regard to His creatures. And she saw how our merciful Creator reconciled the sinners with His glorious father by reminding Him of His many torments.

108. She experienced all these revelations and so many others that she could not tell about and that you could not remember in the time period that we mentioned above. And thus, one night, she had such great visions and such secret revelations of eternal glory that no mortal could describe them or make any one understand them. And the following night she had horrible visions, full of such great pains and terrors that one could not enumerate or give any idea of them, let alone describe them.

Chapter 9. Take Note of the Miracle.

109. Now I will tell you of a great miracle that our Lord God did for her and two others after their death.[2]

110. This saintly creature, Beatrice of Ornacieux, and another woman of the Sassenage family and another one from the Alleman family from Gresivaudan (I could not find out the names of the latter two at the moment I was writing this), supposedly went down from Parmenie with the others sent by the order to Eymeux[3] to found a new convent. Later the nuns left this place because it

---

1 My translation reproduces the kind of breathless enumerative technique used here by Margaret. All the elements of Christ's Passion are strung together with "et" (and).

2 Beatrice died on November 25, 1303

3 Eymeux and the other places mentioned in these stories are in the Isère valley, southwest of the Grande Chartreuse.

was too close to the secular world, and they returned to Parmenie, except for these three women who had already died and had been buried next to each other in the cemetery of the convent at Eymeux.

111. Subsequently—since God arranges things according to His will—several nuns from Parmenie, inspired by our Lord, or by the three nuns, as I believe, went to speak to the prioress and the vicar, named dom Roz de Charis (formerly a monk at Valbonne and today at Sainte-Croix) and told them that one absolutely had to go and fetch the bones of these three saintly creatures, and they also said many other things.

112. When the above-mentioned vicar realized that this had to be done, he went to this place and he had a dangerous and tiring job of it before those who were in charge of the convent at Eymeux were willing to give him what he asked for, and before the bishop of Valence would finally give orders for them to do so. Still, everything came out the way God had ordained.

113. The vicar arrived, he removed the bones of the three saintly creatures, put them in a sack and tied them onto a donkey; as for the bones of the lord of Tullins and of some others, he put them on a horse, and then he left.

114. When he came to the ford at Tèches, he met two squires of the house of the Dauphin who had been there all day (it was noon) because they could not cross the river which had overflowed from its bed; it had rained continuously for three days and three nights. He dined with the two squires. But while he was saying his prayers, before dinner, near the saintly bodies, he told them that if they wanted to be transported to Parmenie they would have to lower the water so that he could cross without danger; otherwise he would take them back to the place from which he had taken them, as he did not have enough money to stay in this place or to go elsewhere.

115. At that moment the rain got even heavier. They quickly had a drink, then he loaded his horse and his donkey, got on the horse and rode towards the river. And everyone told him that if he approached the water everything he had with him would perish. He ordered the guides to have the donkey which was loaded with the three holy bodies step into the water first. And immediately the water went down so far that it seemed to them that the water disappeared into the earth and that the ground emerged. They crossed over to the other side, and the river was almost dry.

116. When the squires saw this, they followed him and they were so stupefied that they had no idea where they were. And right away the water rose again.

117. Shortly before arriving at Tullins, he came upon another mountain stream which had overflowed because of the heavy rains, and which carried along trees and tree stumps torn from the mountainside through which it descends. And near the ford there were three carts full of salt which did not dare to cross.

118. When the vicar saw this, he ordered to have the donkey step into the water first. As soon as the donkey touched the water it receded to such a point that it did not reach higher than one's knee.

119. Then on the same day, at a stream where the water had torn away the plank which served as a bridge, the donkey went by herself off the road to a narrow path winding through the vineyards. When she had advanced about as far as an arrow from a cross-bow would reach, she turned towards the stream and would not move, despite the blows people gave her. When the vicar saw this, he told the guides to look around near the donkey. And they found a large plank which the water had thrown into the bushes, and they put it across the water. When they put it down the donkey voluntarily crossed first and then all the others crossed as well.

120. She left this world on the day of Saint Catherine, that is, the seventh day before the calends of december.[1]

121. Another miracle was told to me by brother Henri of Salins, prior of Bonlieu, an honest and very pious man, and of great perfection. He assured me that he was certain of what I am now going to tell. It is the same story as the one told by dom Jean of Pomeranz, a monk of the Vaucluse region, who was at that time in the house of the order at Parmenie. During Lent, this saintly creature, lady Beatrice of Ornacieux, had mortified herself so much for the love of our Lord and in remembrance of His glorious Passion that, once Good Friday had arrived, her strength was almost completely failing. When the prioress realized this, she had her guarded in a separate room by another lady—strong, prudent and intelligent—so that she could pray and meditate but would not mortify herself beyond reason.

122. When the night of Good Friday arrived she fell asleep very deeply just before matins. When the lady in charge of guarding her saw that she was so deeply asleep, she went to matins just when

---

1 This paragraph is written in smaller letters in the manuscript. It does not fit into the chronology since the events just recounted took place after Beatrice's death. The seventh day before the calends of December is November 25. In the Middle Ages dates were generally given with relation to the calends (beginning of month) and the ides (middle of the month), usually counting backwards, as Margaret does here.

they were beginning to sing in church; she locked the door and took the key with her.

123. Somewhat later, she woke up and heard that the other ladies were singing in church; she reflected that on such a day she should really serve our Lord and called for her companion. When she realized that she was not there, she got up and began to pray to Our Lady: "Sweetest Lady, mother of the Creator of all creatures, who, in order to give a new life to His creatures, suffered on this day death and torments, and you yourself, sweetest Lady, you were a martyr in the spirit while watching the pains and sufferings borne by Him without any reason, I beg of you, for the pity that you felt for your dear Son and Lord, that if my service has ever pleased you and still pleases you, you will let me go and celebrate the memory of your dear Son, my true Lord God and spouse; in the way that may please your dear Son, please lead me to my sisters in church".

124. Then she took an image of Our Lady that was painted on a piece of wood and put it through the hole in the door and said: "Now I will see, sweetest Lady, if you want me to stay here all alone." At these words she found herself on the other side of the door, without the door having opened, and it remained locked as before. Then she replaced the image of Our Lady in the opening[1] and went to matins at her proper place (in church).

125. When the prioress and the others saw her there, they were stupefied and some of them ran to see whether she had broken the door; but they found it well locked and the image in the opening inside. Then they were even more stupefied. When the vicar and the prioress arrived they ordered her in the name of the obedience she owed them to confess how she had gotten out. And she confessed everything exactly the way it has just been told.

Letters

From a Letter

126. To her dearest brother and dearly beloved father in God, his poor sister, salvation and eternal love for Him whose goodness sustains the saintly souls who are in heaven etc.[2]

127. Dearest brother, you have asked me to let you know what kind of penance you should do for the wrongs you have done our

---

1 This opening must be a kind of niche in the door, probably the exact size of the image.
2 This first paragraph is a formulaic greeting and therefore has no verb. One does not know to whom it is addressed.

sweet Creator; but I do not very well how to inform you because it would be so much better for me to tell you directly than to have to write it down. Nonetheless, I will let you know how the person who loves you most in the world has done it.[1]

128. When I realized that you did not understand these things very well, I began to act just as He had taught me.

129. When the day of the Nativity of Jesus Christ came, I spiritually took the glorious child into my arms. Thus I carried and kissed Him tenderly in the arms of my heart,[2] from the hour of matins until tierce.[3] Then I went to relax for a little bit and I thought of putting some order into the things weighing on my poor heart.

130. At noon, I reflected how my sweet Lord was tormented for our sins and suspended all naked from the cross between two thieves. When I came to the point where the evil people had deserted Him, I went towards Him, with great respect, and removed the nails; then I took Him upon my shoulders and took Him down from the cross and put Him in the arms of my heart; and it seemed to me that I carried Him as easily as if He had been one year old. If I told you the other great consolation that I experienced through Him, you would hardly be able to understand it.

131. In the evening when I was going to lie down, in my spirit I put Him down on my bed and I kissed His tender hands and these blessed feet which were so cruelly pierced for our sins. And then I bent down towards that glorious flank which was so cruelly wounded for me. And there I commended myself and my brother to Him and asked forgiveness for our sins; and thus I rested until matins, and this went on from the Nativity to the day of the Purification of Our Lady.[4]

132. If our Lord gave you the grace to do the same, I truly believe that He would be more content of this for you than for me. I could not write to you everything I wanted to, because I did not feel comfortable writing at all etc.

---

1 It is not quite clear what Margaret refers to here.
2 That is, not her physical arms. Although the experience seems to be described in physical terms, it is actually purely spiritual.
3 That is, from about 3 a.m. to 9 a.m.
4 The Bible specified a forty-day purification period after childbirth. The date of the Purification of the Virgin is February 2. See Luke 2:22.

From Another Letter

133. My sweet father, you have asked me to write to you what you put into the pages of your little book. I do not recall very well what that was, unless it was a sentence which should be at the end of the judgment in the following form:[1] "I think that if the king of France had an only son who was destined to be king after him, and if the son through his folly had done something that is punishable by death, and if the king were so just that he felt he had to punish him and throw him with his own hands into a burning furnace, then that would be extremely painful for him. Imagine then God's great anguish when He will have to throw so many sons and daughters into the fires of hell and to abandon them."

134. I do not know whether this is what you wanted. You will find these things put down more correctly in the great books which belong to the prior of Liget.[2]

135. Dearest father, you informed me that in the passage on the Passion you found some things that are not written in the Holy Scriptures. In particular, you find that He was hit on the head with a bowl and that the bowl broke from the violent blow. You should know that I heard this preached by a superior of the Franciscans, in the middle of a sermon. And I believe that he would not have said it if he had not somehow known about it, for he had the reputation of being a good scholar and a worthy man.

136. My dearest father, I did not write this to give to you or anyone else, nor did I write this so that it would remain after my death, for I am not a person who should write things that last or that should be considered important. I only wrote these things so that I could concentrate my thoughts on them while my heart was occupied with the things of this world, and so that I could turn my heart towards my Creator and away from the world.

137. My sweet father, I do not know whether the things that are written in the book are in the Holy Scriptures, but I know that she who put them in writing was one night so enraptured by our Lord that it seemed to her that she saw all these things. And when she came back to her senses, she had all these things written in her heart in such a way that she could think of nothing else, and

---

1 Most likely, Margaret is writing to someone who had been visiting her convent and had, on that occasion, seen some of her (now lost) writings. Perhaps he is asking her to elaborate on some notes he had taken at that time.

2 It is not known what exactly these "great books" were. The charterhouse of Saint John of Liget was in Loches near Tours. At the time that Margaret was writing the prior was named Philip. He was prior until 1312 and died in 1315.

her heart was so full that she could not eat, drink or sleep until she was so weak that the doctors thought she was on the point of death.

138. She thought that if she put these things into writing in the same way that our Lord had put them into her heart, her heart would be unburdened. She began to write everything that is in this book, in the order that it was in her heart; and as soon as she had put the words into the book, everything left her heart. And when she had written everything down, she was all cured. I firmly believe that if she had not put all this down in writing, she would have died or gone mad, because for seven days she had neither slept nor eaten and she had never before done anything to get her into such a state. And this is why I believe that all this was written down through the will of our Lord.

139. My sweet father, I tell you that I am so occupied with the business of our house that I cannot think of those things that are good, for I have so much to do that I do not know where to turn first. We did not harvest the wheat in the seventh month of the year, and our vineyards are devastated by a storm. In addition, our church is in such bad repair that we have to rebuild it in part, etc.

Another Letter

140. My dearest father, as for myself, I cannot give you anything that would console you, but I am sending you [the account of] a very sweet and comforting thing that happened to a certain person not long ago, for I do not want your servant to have come to me for nothing. I ask you to keep it secret, for the person who had this vision does not want it made public in any manner whatsoever.

141. Not long ago a person I know[1] began to pray at the hour of tierce and to meditate on the great goodness of our Lord. She was not very conscious of anything, and it seemed to her that she was transported to heaven and that she saw Jesus Christ sitting on His throne. And around Him there was a group of very beautiful people, among them popes, bishops and archbishops, kings and other people, and lords without number, who were all looking at His very noble face. In front of this large group was another, made up of a different kind of people, who were all standing, performing

---

1   Undoubtedly Margaret herself. Like Paul in 2. Cor.12:2-4 ("I know a man..."), as we noted earlier, Margaret speaks of her own visions in this indirect manner.

holy services and singing in front of Jesus Christ and His attendants. They were singing: " 'Let the righteous be joyful',"[1] with
such great sweetness that one could not think nor tell about it.

142. This person came back to her senses and she thought that
this was what was written in Daniel: "A thousand thousands
served him."[2] And this was at the hour of noon. She was very much
comforted by this vision and , after the hour of nones had passed,
she still seemed to hear this sweet singing that she had heard
earlier. If only Jesus Christ could make you hear it in the way that
I want you to! Amen.

Another Letter

143. Not long ago some good people were together in a house
and spoke of God. There was a worthy man who said that once he
had asked a lady what the word "vehement" meant and that the
lady had answered that it meant "strong." There was a person
present who was deeply touched by this word, and it seemed to her
that all this was of great importance, but she never dared to ask
him to explain the word "vehement" to her.

144. Nonetheless she subsequently asked a lot of people what
that word meant, but she could find no one who could answer her
to her satisfaction. This word was so deeply driven into her heart
that she could not get rid of it, not while she was praying nor under
any other circumstances, until she finally addressed a fervent
prayer to our Lord that He in His great goodness may teach her
what this word meant and remove it from her heart.

145. Before she had finished her prayers, the one who is filled
with sweetness and pity wanted to comfort her and to draw her
spirit towards Him; and He did this in such a way that it seemed
to her that she was in a large deserted open space where there was
only one high mountain, and at the foot of this mountain there
stood a marvellous tree. This tree had five branches which were
all dry and were bending downwards. On the leaves of the first
branch there was written "sight"; on the second was written
"hearing"; on the third was written "taste"; on the fourth was
written "smell"; on the fifth was written "touch."[3] On the top of the
tree there lay a large circle, similar to the bottom of a barrel, which

---

1 In Latin in the text. This is the beginning of Psalm 67:4 (68:3).
2 Also in Latin in the text. Daniel 7:10. This is part of Daniel's famous vision of the four
   beasts which is linked to the visions of the end of the world in the Apocalypse. Daniel, of
   course, is not speaking of Jesus but of "one that was ancient of days" and whose "raiment
   was white as snow, and the hair of his head [was] like pure wool" (Daniel 7:9).
3 The words designating the five senses are in Latin in the text. The tree seems to represent
   the human faculties in a state of decay without the grace of Christ.

covered the tree completely so that neither the sun nor the dew-drops could get to it.

146. And after she had looked attentively at the tree, she raised her eyes towards the mountain, and she saw a great stream descending with a force like that of the sea. This stream rushed so violently onto the bottom of this tree that all its roots were turned upside down and the top was stuck in the earth; and the branches which had been bent downwards were now stretching towards heaven. And the leaves which had been dry were all green, and the roots which had been in the earth were all spread out and pointing towards the sky; and they were all green and full of leaves as branches usually are.

147. My dearest and honored lady, I write to you to report a great favor that our Lord did for a certain person not long ago.

148. A good five years ago a nun was so gravely ill that she could not go to church nor say her prayers as she usually did. She was in bed and very vexed, and she prayed to our Lord with insistence to send her some comfort in His grace. On that prayer she fell asleep and it seemed to her that she was looking into the sky towards the east, and that she saw there a beautiful gate, as splendid as the sun. On this gate there were five precious stones, all red like beautiful rubies: between two of the stones there was a distance of at least six feet, the third was in the middle of the gate, and the others were above that at a distance of about a foot from each other.

149. She thought anyone who could enter through this gate would be blessed. At the moment when she least thought of it, she seemed to see Jesus Christ in the center of the gate, His arms and hands outstretched: the two red stones above Him penetrated His blessed hands, the stone in the middle penetrated His blessed side, and the two stones from below penetrated His blessed feet.

150. And while she was watching these marvellous events, a voice told her: "I, Jesus Christ, am the gate; if you want to enter you have to pass through me."[1] She woke up and her heart was filled with great joy, great sweetness and great compassion for the pitiful wounds she had seen. She diligently thought about how she could best serve Jesus Christ.

151. She resolved in her heart that from now on she would always say fifty "Our Fathers" in the memory of the Passion of Jesus Christ and His blessed wounds. And she divided up these

---

1   The description of the gate seems to be a visual rendering of John 10:9: "I am the door; if any one enters by me, he will be saved...."

"our Fathers" so that she said five in honor of His blessed head and hair, so violently washed and beaten for us; then she said five in memory of His blessed eyes because He looked at her with such pity; then she said five in memory of His sweet ears which had to listen to so many outrages for us; then she said five in honor of His blessed nose, so that He would give her the grace to smell something of her great sweetness with which she loved Him tenderly; then she said five in memory of His blessed mouth so that He would give her His benediction and call her into His kingdom; then she said five in memory of the wound in His side, so that He would wash and bless her with this fountain springing from His side; then she said five for each hand, so that with the strength of His arms He would protect and defend her against her enemies.; then she said five more for each wound on His feet, so that Jesus Christ would forgive her for her sins as He had forgiven the Magdalen.[1]

152. Not long ago this person said these "Our Fathers" in honor of the Passion, and she thought that it would have been good, after having washed the wounds of Christ spiritually, to anoint them with some precious balm, as the Magdalen had done. She felt the wounds of Jesus Christ so deeply in her heart that she seemed to see Him before her all covered with wounds. But she could not imagine with what she could anoint Him, and she begged Him to show her how to do it.

153. Shortly after that it seemed to her that a voice told her: "The thing that brings me the greatest comfort and sweetness is a devout prayer, said in the purity of heart and the peace of conscience". She thought she would never leave off saying these "Our Fathers," for it seemed to her that this was the best prayer one could say.

Some Stories

Note the Prophecy

154. When Monsieur Henri de Villars, archbishop of Lyons, was in Rome on some business for the church of Lyons, he sent, some time before his death,[2] a letter (written by himself) to Monsieur Guichard of Ars whom Margaret of Oingt, prioress of Poleteins, asked whether he knew anything of Monseigneur the archbishop.

---

1 Saint Mary Magdalene was the prototype of the converted sinner who was then blessed with special graces. She was said to have ministered to Christ in Galilee and stood next to the cross at the Crucifixion. She discovered with two other women the empty tomb and heard the announcement of the Resurrection. The "woman who had a bad name" mentioned in Luke 7:37 was believed to have been Mary Magdalene.

2 He died in 1301.

He answered very freely that yes, he knew something, and showed her the letter that he had received two days earlier. "I must tell you," she said, "that yesterday he was in the most beautiful company he ever was, and shortly he will be in a company even more beautiful and honorable."

155. When she had said this she left the knight [Guichard of Ars], because she could no longer hold back her tears; she did not want to say anything else to the knight. But the knight made a note of what she had said and of the day, and it turned out that at that moment, Monsieur the Archbishop had just died.

Another Notable Story

156. It also happened another time that that same Guichard of Ars, the knight, and Monsieur Henri, his brother, a canon from Lyons, went to exhume the bodies of their father and mother, and of some other relatives and friends who had all been buried in the cemetery of Poleteins. They wanted to put them all into a tomb that they had built in that church or very near to it.

157. There were several very honorable people: bishops, abbots and priors and many other worthy people. When the moment came when the remains of those who were buried in the cemetery were unearthed, the prioress Margaret had all the bones brought to her. And she handled these bones with her bare hands and everyone present was quite dumbfounded by what she did and said; for in everyone's presence she said that the skull of one of her nuns[1] was missing (she had been the first cousin of Monsieur Guichard of Ars and of Monsieur Henri of Ars and had been buried in the same tomb with her father). And there was no one who knew how many bodies there were in this tomb, not Madame Margaret nor anyone else. In any case, the first time five skulls were brought.

158. At that point she sent people back to look for the skull of the nun, whom as far as I know, she had never seen; she had only heard that a nun was buried there. And the nun's skull was found and brought before her. And she said that this was really the skull of this nun. It thus was made manifest that this glorious creature had the Holy Spirit within her, regarding all the things that had been done and that had to be done.

---

1   As it turns out in paragraph 158, Margaret had not known this nun. Consequently, "one of her nuns" must mean a nun who had at one time in the past been at Margaret's Charterhouse of Poleteins.

Another Notable Story

159. A short time before his death, dom Durand, vicar of the Cell of Our Lady and a monk at the Charterhouse monastery, for the love of God and for charity asked her[1] for some gift or favor. He asked because he knew that she was a saintly creature. She answered him: "The next time when you will see me."

160. He never saw her again in this mortal life. But after she had died, he was asleep one night and it seemed to him (or at least he thought so) that a dove, whiter than anything he had ever seen, came to him and put its beak into his mouth; and it left behind such great glory and such great sweetness that he could never tell about it. For three days he could not eat or drink anything whatsoever because everything seemed so bitter to him in comparison to the great sweetness that he had experienced. When he woke up he thought that this had been sister Margaret, or rather the second Saint Margaret,[2] who had condescended to visiting him, as she had promised.

---

1   That is, Margaret.
2   He means Margaret in her new, or second, form as saint. Or, since there already was a Saint Margaret, he may call her the "second Saint Margaret" for that reason.

Essay

The Idea of Writing As Authority and Conflict In the Works of Margaret of Oingt[1]

What did it mean to write as a woman in the Middle Ages? For the majority of writing women it meant to compose religious works. Looking back over the centuries, one finds only a handful of women who wrote secular narrative or poetry. In the twelfth century, there was Marie de France—but nothing but her name is known about her. Then there were the female troubadours, or "trobaritz,"—but after the thirteenth century, one hears no more about female secular poets. Christine de Pizan, one of the most interesting and productive writers of the late Middle Ages, remained an exception. Browsing through the fascinating anthologies of Peter Dronke and Katharina Wilson we find few examples of non-religious writing. This is hardly surprising, for being able to write presupposed a relatively high level of education and, except for the nobility, women only had access to education in the convent. Universities were (except in Italy) categorically closed to women. But even in the convent, education was a privilege: lower-class women seldom benefited from educational opportunities. They remained what they had been in the outside world: the servants of others. Consequently writing, particularly in Latin, was circumscribed by both class and gender. But while lower-class men had more possibilities to rise through a clerkly education, lower-class women did not. They could gain authority, however, through visionary experiences, even if they could not write them down themselves and had to dictate them.

In the history of women's literature religious writing should not take second place to secular narrative and poetry. In fact, some of the most beautiful medieval lyrics were composed by religious women. To name just two: Hrotsvit of Gandersheim (ca. 932-1000)

---

1 Quotes from Margaret's works will be given in parenthetical form indicating the text and the paragraph. P=*A Page of Meditations*; M=*Mirror*; B=*Life of Beatrice of Ornacieux*; L+S=*Letters and Stories*.

was an extremely learned German poet who wrote legends, dramas and epics; and Hadewijch of Brabant in the thirteenth century composed many poems that rank among the most accomplished and innovative works of her time.

Although most female religious writers purported to write unmediated accounts of their visions and mystical experiences, they were also part of a literary tradition which, together with the visions themselves, provided the authoritative basis for women's mystical writing.

In the twelfth century, Saint Bernard of Clairvaux had found new ways of writing about his love of Christ and the Virgin Mary. His works, especially his commentary on the *Song of Songs* with its striking nuptial imagery, strongly influenced female mysticism and its expression. Most of his writings were known to women in abridgments or adaptations, but this fact did not diminish his reputation of being a "mellifluous" speaker. Bernard thus functioned as a stylistic model for mystical writers, but at the same time he evoked an ardent love that in its expression sometimes equaled the love these women had for Christ Himself. Thus Gertrud of Helfta had a vision of the saint in which he was dressed in garments of three colors: white for his virginal purity; violet for his perfect life; and red for "glowing love." Mechthild, whom we encountered in the Introduction, had a similar vision. But the most intense experience was reserved for Margaretha Ebner who in a very graphic vision kissed and hugged Saint Bernard with "great lust and desire."[1]

This type of experience—whether the vision featured Saint Bernard or Christ, both of them writers or teachers—combines the two strands of authority that we outlined earlier: the grace of a vision fused with writerly skill allowed women to become "authors." Caroline Bynum has shown how women could create new and different bases for authority through their visions of the Eucharist: in their visions they could assume a priestly function that would be closed to them in real life.[2] In addition, as Elizabeth Petroff points out,

---

1 For a balanced account of Saint Bernard's influence on female mysticism see Ulrich Köpf, "Bernhard von Clairvaux in der Frauenmystik," pp. 48-77 in Dinzelbacher and Bauer, eds. *Frauenmystik im Mittelalter*. Pp. 66-67 for the visions of Saint Bernard. Also J. Wimsatt, "St. Bernard, the Canticle of Canticles, and Medieval Piety," pp. 77-96 in Szarmach, ed.

2 For this argument see *Jesus as Mother*, ch. 5.

even the most contemplative women were often active reformers in their communities. In their meditations and visions, they were regularly developing new values for the feminine, for Christ, for human experience, and in their writings they developed new uses of language to speak of all this.[1]

In this context, visions take the place of priestly ordination and the kind of authority that an elevated rank in the ecclesiastical hierarchy would bring for men even without the special grace of mystical revelations. Visions thus constituted the special empowerment of the mystical writer.

But writing was not only related to authority, it could also be a source of conflict. The most common sign of this conflict is the mystical writer's reluctance to record her experiences. Inadequacy, fear and lack of education are some of the reasons cited by various women.[2] (This fear undoubtedly explains the frequency with which these women refer to themselves in the third person.) Julian of Norwich, for example, cautions

But God forbid that you should say or assume that I am a teacher, for that is not and never was my intention; for I am a woman, ignorant, weak and, frail. But I know very well that what I am saying I have received at the revelation of him who is the sovereign teacher.[3]

And St. Umiltà says

I am amazed and fearful and ashamed concerning these things, which I dare to write and dictate, for I have not read them in other books, nor have I ever applied myself to learning human knowledge; but only the spirit of God has spoken in me...[4]

Nevertheless, the female mystic feels compelled to write because the knowledge of her experiences could be profitable for others. A good example is the fourteenth-century mystic Christina Ebner who always kept her potential readers in mind and even occasionally interrupted her visions so that they could be written down![5]

1 *Medieval Women's Visionary Literature*, p. 21.
2 The reluctance to write is one of the list of common traits among women mystics found by Valerie Lagorio. See "Mysticism, Christian. Continental (Women)," pp.8-17 in *The Dictionary of the Middle Ages*, vol. 9 (1987).
3 *Julian of Norwich's Showings*. Transl. E. Colledge and J. Walsh. Cited in Petroff, p. 27.
4 Cited by Petroff, p. 27.
5 See Siegfried Ringler, "Die Rezeption mittelalterlicher Frauenmystik," pp. 178-200 in Dinzelbacher and Bauer, eds.; p. 189.

More than a direct transcription of visionary experience, mystical writings are *literary texts* with a specific purpose and structure. When women choose to write in the first person, the "I" of these texts is not so much an autobiographical or experiential "I" but rather a literary "I," created expressly in order to relate the experience. This first-person narrator is part of her culture. Many of the images she uses have their direct origin in the art and literature of her time. There are many examples of visionaries who saw the Virgin Mary just as she could be seen as a statue of their church, or the infant Jesus just as He was depicted in an illuminated manuscript the nun had been perusing.

On the one hand, writing—grounded as it is in tradition—is emancipation; but on the other, because this tradition was mostly male, it is threatening. The woman has to assert herself, usurp a male prerogative in making her voice heard.

But there is another source of conflict in mystical writing, and that is the fundamental paradox of writing about mystical experiences at all: by their very nature mystical visions are mysteries, a privileged view of God's deepest secrets. They *cannot* be directly commmunicated. To say the "unsayable" is thus the task of the mystical writer.[1] Women who dictated their visions escaped, to a certain extent, from this conflictual situation. But women like Margaret of Oingt, who wrote themselves—and not only in Latin but also in her own vernacular, Francoprovençal—lived this conflict intensely. This explains Margaret's frequent and imaginative use of metaphors and images related to writing. This imagery is central to her thought: it reveals her sources of strength, her fears and her ultimate restraint and modesty in face of the extraordinary gifts God had given her.

The title of her first work, *A Page of Meditations*, indicates that Margaret thought in terms of a text, a "page." It signals the literary or bookish character of her meditations. This idea is reinforced by the way the meditation is triggered: by a biblical verse, that is a *citation* from the scriptures (P1). Her meditation is thus, in a sense, exegesis, or interpretation of the scriptures. We recall that in the Carthusian order female religious were allowed to read aloud from the scriptures for others: Margaret could very well have read to her sisters during the evening meal. Right away then, her medita-

---

1   For a complex analysis of the paradox of mystical speaking see Walter Haug "Zur Grundlegung einer Theorie mystischen Sprechens," pp. 494-508 in Kurt Ruh, ed. *Abendländische Mystik des Mittelalters.*

tion has a didactic function. It serves as a model for the right way of using the scriptures: as a point of departure for pious thoughts.

Paragraph 4 is crucial for an understanding of Margaret's attitude toward writing. Writing here is seen as a kind of purgation for an overflowing heart. Margaret is so filled by the thoughts of God's sweetness and goodness that she is torn between removing them, so that she can feel relieved, and to keep contemplating them, so that she can relive the sweetness of grace. She finally finds a reason for writing them down:

> I thought that the hearts of men and women are so
> flighty that they can hardly ever remain in one place,
> and because of that I fixed in writing the thoughts that
> God had ordered into my heart.

This way she will not lose the precious thoughts and she will be able to think them over at her leisure. Here she clearly defines the function of her text: it is a transcription of a meditation, but at the same time it can be the basis for countless repetitions of this meditation. Indeed, she defines the beginning and the end of meditation in terms of writing: the time it took her to write this down, she says, is the time she spent meditating on her sins. The equation between meditation and writing could not be more clearly expressed.

Nonetheless, like other mystical women, Margaret begs for forgiveness for the "presumption" she displays in writing down her thoughts. She has "no sense or learning," her model text is God's grace. She thus posits herself as a copier. We know that one of the important activities of medieval religious was the copying of manuscripts. The Latin word *exemplar* she uses here is thus highly significant: it designates the original manuscript that a scribe was copying from. Margaret sees herself in a kind of spiritual *scriptorium*, or copying workshop, in which she is nothing but the careful transcriber of a model—and this model is God's grace. The entire process of divine inspiration and expression is circumscribed by the terminology of manuscript production: Margaret is God's writer.

But although Margaret has God's grace as her model or *exemplar*, she again fears that she is presumptuous. She is a "small worm" who has the audacity to speak of Christ's marvels (P8). She "cannot speak of" all God's kindnesses. Here Margaret confronts the necessity of speaking the unspeakable. Already in the New Testament, the paradox of speaking about mystical visions or raptures was evident. Paul says in 2. Corinthians 12:3-4

> And I know that this man was caught up into
> Paradise—whether in the body or out of the body I do

not know, God knows—and he heard things that cannot
be told, which man cannot utter.

And yet, Margaret will tell, particularly in the *Mirror* and in the
Life of Beatrice of Ornacieux, of the most splendid visions and
revelations.

One way of evading the problem of the presumption and the
audacity of writing—and at the same time to assert its authen-
ticity—is to adopt the role of mere transcriber. This is what
Margaret does at the end of the *Page of Meditations* when she says

Sweet Lord, write into my heart what you want me to
do. Write your law, write there your orders so that they
will never be erased. (P109)

We recall that this text, written in Latin, was among the ones
brought to and sanctioned by the Chapter General of the Carthusians in 1294, thus helping to establish her authority as a
visionary. Without questioning the sincerity of Margaret's voice,
we can say that she was a skillful rhetorician. She used the topoi
of modesty, of being nothing but a mouthpiece for God's word so
successfully that her male superiors approved of her—the first and
only female mystical writer of her order.

Margaret's visions become more dazzling as she is received into
the orthodox mainstream of mystical writing. It almost seems as
if the official sanction of her activities opened the floodgates of her
imagination. The term "imagination" is not in any way derogatory;
but one has to make a distinction between different types of
mystical writing. As we saw in the Introduction, Master Eckhart,
the famous German mystic, devalued the intensely emotional
mystical experiences typical of women at the expense of specula-
tive mysticism, in his opinion more typical of male writing. Of
course, there were some women, like Margaret Porete, the author
of the *Mirror of Simple Souls*, who stressed the theoretical aspects
of mysticism more than its emotional side. But on the whole,
intellectual speculation and philosophical thought were not the
hallmarks of the mystical writers of Margaret's generation. While
in the first generation of female mystics, such as Hildegard of
Bingen (d. 1179) and Elisabeth of Schönau (d. 1164), prophecy had
dominated as a form of mystical experience, the second generation
stressed mystical union and *imitatio Christi*, that is the reenactment of the Passion. This second generation was especially
prominent in the regions of what would today be Belgium, Holland
and Germany, as well as in Northern Italy. In France, there were
very few female mystics. Scholars only name Douceline of Digne

(d. 1274), Beatrice of Ornacieux and Margaret of Oingt.[1] Two out of the three French mystics can be heard in this volume!

Was Margaret aware of the importance of her voice? Of the fact that she almost singlehandedly established a French tradition of mystical writing? These questions are difficult to answer because Margaret never abandons her stance of modesty. But the fact that her visions became more magnificent, that she wrote the Life of a contemporary woman saint, and that—after her first work—she did all this in the vernacular reveal a confidence in her writing, an authority that no longer needs male approval.

The *Page of Meditations* had ended with Margaret's prayer to the Lord to write His commands into her heart. The *Mirror* opens with a similar image: "By the grace of our Lord, this creature had written into her heart the holy life that Jesus had led on earth" (M2). This image of writing calls forth another one, one that dominates the first two parts of the *Mirror*: the vision of Christ with a closed book in His hand. In the description of the significance of the book's colors we note a skilfull transposition from Christ's book to her own heart. Margaret describes what was written in the white letters: "the saintly life of the blessed Son of God" (M4). This, of course, is exactly what she herself had "written into her heart." A similar equivalency between her own heart and the book in the vision appears in paragraph 7 where Margaret says "After she had looked into this book carefully, she began to read in the book of her conscience which she found full of falsity and lies." She sees her own character as the contrary of what she finds in the life of Christ. One could imagine the page of the book in the vision inscribed by a forceful pen: what appears on the reverse side of the page will be the opposite of what is on the *recto* side.[2] Thus Margaret presents her life as the *verso* to Christ's *recto*—all within the wider imagery of reading and writing in the heart.

As Margaret compared her own conscience to what she found in the white letters, she can now test her patience in the tribulations she finds in the black letters (M9). Her education continues in the red letters in which she learns to enjoy suffering (M10). The gold letters finally make her "desire the things of heaven" (M11).

---

1 For a good overview of female mysticism see Peter Dinzelbächer,"Europaische Frauenmystik: Ein Überblick" pp. 11-23 in Dinzelbacher and Bauer, eds. See p. 19 for the list of French women mystics. The indispensable anthology with excellent introductions is Elizabeth Petroff, *Medieval Women's Visionary Literature*.

2 *Recto* and *verso* are the technical terms used to designate the two sides of a page, or *folio*. The right side was usually much smoother than the reverse because of the nature of the parchment (the flesh vs. the fur side of the animal skin).

Margaret's increased understanding of herself and of God's will is a reading process; but at the same time it is a writing process, because as she reads she writes down her thoughts for us.

The ambiguity of the book (is it only part of her vision or is it a physical object?) is quite striking. She is looking at her book, it opens unexpectedly (M14)—is this a vision or is it an experience of her imagination, in her thoughts? One cannot expect clear-cut answers to these questions. As Peter Dinzelbacher points out with regard to other women mystics: "Do we not always find in Mechthild of Magdeburg, in Angela of Foligno, a mixture of visions and prayers, of real and imagined experiences?"[1]

Whatever the status of the book between Margaret's visions, it reenters her vision in paragraph 15 where it opens for the first time: "The inside of this book was like a beautiful mirror." Mirror, of course, is also the title of her work. Earlier she had equated her inscribed heart with the book of the vision, and now she seems to suggest a relation between her own *Mirror* and the inside of the book. It is here that Margaret develops the theme of the "unspeakable" in a series of claims that what she sees in the book cannot be expressed:

> Of the things she saw in this book I will tell you only little, for I have neither the understanding that could conceive of it, nor the mouth which could tell it. (M15) …but there is no human mouth that could speak of it. (M16) …no human heart could imagine it. (M17) There is no human intelligence that could imagine… (M22) …no human heart could conceive of it. (M24)

In a sense, these statements spell out the capitulation of the Christian writer in face of God's overwhelming grace and beauty. They also mark the effort of finding a language that will do justice to the greatest secrets. "A new song"—this is what is needed, and Margaret describes such a song in her vision:

> [The angels and saints] sing a song that is all new and of such sweetness that it is a wonderful melody…. And this song is hardly finished when they start another one, also all new. And this song will last forever. (M18)

The saints, as well, cannot fully comprehend God's goodness (M20); they are thus in the same position as Margaret. But they all sing the "new song," a term which shows that only a new language will serve the mystical writer.

---

1 Dinzelbacher, "Europäische Frauenmystik," p. 13.

"Mirror," or *speculum*, was also the technical term used to describe an important genre of writing: didactic works of a comprehensive nature. The genre was especially popular in the thirteenth century when Vincent of Beauvais (d. 1264) wrote his *Speculum maius* (consisting of the *Speculum historiale*, *Speculum doctrinale* and *Speculum naturale*) which in 9885 chapters tried to sum up the knowledge of Vincent's time. This meaning of the term "mirror" has to be kept in mind because Margaret surely understood it in this way. A mirror reflects and through this reflection it teaches.

The most striking element of this mirror imagery appears in a later vision which takes Margaret to a "brilliant" place full of "beautiful and glorious people" (M23). There Jesus Christ appears to her and His body functions as a mirror:

This glorious body was so noble and so transparent that one could clearly see the soul inside of it. The body was so noble that one could see oneself reflected in it, more clearly than in a mirror. (M24)

The transparency of the mirror that allows a view of the soul evokes ideas of the magic of mirrors which, in Greek antiquity for example, were believed to hold captive the viewer's soul. Magical mirrors made apperances in contemporary romances, and although Margaret's use of the mirror imagery is anything but pagan and she is firmly rooted in the Christian tradition of writing, her readers may have found some echoes of more popular currents of thought.

The last link in the chain of mirror images appears towards the end of Margaret's text:

He made them (His friends) so beautiful and so glorious that each of them sees the Trinity in himself, as one sees in a beautiful mirror that which is in front of it. (M35)

This is of course the ultimate grace: to become a mirror that reflects the Trinity.

What is most important here is Margaret's creation of a series of equivalencies involving the term "mirror." First, there is her own text; then the book in her vision; next, the body of Jesus Christ; and finally, the Trinity: there is a movement upwards in the heavenly hierarchy, but the basis for this movement is provided by Margaret's writing, her *Mirror*; whatever is taught in these different mirrors follows from her initial scriptural impulse.

Teaching, particularly teaching by example, is also one of the principal goals of a saint's life, but the teaching is more implicit here than in the *Mirror*. At the beginning of the *Life of Beatrice of*

Ornacieux Margaret states that she writes in the honor of God. Thus Margaret as a writer subordinates herself completely to the higher task of conveying the saintliness and the exemplary character of Beatrice's life.

Beatrice, like Margaret, had visionary experiences, but unlike in the *Mirror* where seeing and speaking subject were identical, here it is Beatrice who sees and Margaret who speaks. The discursive situation is thus completely different and explains the many instances when Margaret states that Beatrice's visions cannot be adequately written about: here the theme of the "unspeakable" dominates. This is especially true later in the *Life*, in chapter 5 for example, where Margaret says about Beatrice's vision of paradise: "She never wanted to reveal of this vision anything but the fact that she could neither describe nor understand it" (B82); or at the beginning and the end of the eucharistic vision: "She could not describe nor make anyone understand (His great beauty)" (B85, B86). At other times, it is Beatrice who refuses to speak about her visions: "...she saw and learned many secrets of our Lord that she never wanted to talk about" (B96). The theme of the "unspeakable" culminates in Beatrice's last visions

> ...she had such great visions and such secret revelations of eternal glory that no mortal could describe them or make anyone understand them. And the following night she had horrible visions, full of such great pains and terrors that one could not enumerate them, let alone describe them. (B108)

Nonetheless, the great vision of chapter 4 is a beautiful example of the poetry generated by mystical experiences. Yet, the vision is not enough in itself: it needs to be interpreted. Christ tells Beatrice: "I will give you understanding of all things at another time" (B78). Much later, Margaret informs us,

> in these visions was revealed to her the significance of the gold cloth and the twelve stones...And the sig-

nificance of what He said to her was also revealed...And
it was explained to her what He said. (B102)

The vision is thus posited as a *text* that calls forth its own interpretation.[1] And it is Christ Himself who glosses, interprets the
vision that He Himself had sent her and had appeared in. True to
His role in the gospels, Christ as a kind of glossator, participates
in the process that characterized medieval writing, and not only
in the religious domain: the establishment of text *and* gloss.[2]

The theme of writing also appears frequently in Margaret's
letters. In the first of her letters Margaret takes up some of the
points that opened her *Page of Meditations*: the topoi of humility
and modesty, of an unwillingness to write and the idea that writing
is a cure for an overflowing of the heart.

"I could not write to you everything I wanted to, because I did
not feel comfortable writing at all" (L+S132), she writes to her
"dearest brother," a Carthusian of whom we do not know the name.
But although Margaret says "I am not a person who should write
things that last or that should be considered important" (L+S136),
she does find an important justification for writing: so that she can
concentrate on pious thoughts while being occupied by the things
of the world.

She insists on the inevitability of writing when she says that
after a vision "she came back to her senses (and) she had all these
things written in her heart" (L+S137). She then unburdens her
heart by "emptying" it, that is, by writing, or transcribing, everything that is in her heart into this book (L+S138). The image of the
"spiritual scriptorium" that we evoked earlier comes to mind here.
Margaret again presents herself as a "copier" of Christ's revelations: the contents of her heart, sent to her by Christ, becomes the
book. Like bloodletting, a very common medical procedure in the

---

1 In secular literature as well, there are examples of the glossing and interpreting of
visions, dreams, and revelations. The thirteenth-century anonymous prose romance the
Queste del saint graal (Quest of the holy grail; ed. Pauphilet), often linked to Cistercian
spirituality, features countless visions sent by God to various knights. These visions are
then interpreted by hermits and other saintly characters. The idea that visions require an
interpretation was certainly part of medieval culture: hence the innumerable glosses on
holy texts.

2 In medieval manuscripts one often finds a small portion of text in the center of the page
surrounded by passages of glosses in smaller writing which are many times as long as the
text itself.

Middle Ages, the transcribing of what is in her heart purges her heart's burden. The text heals:

> And when she had written everything down she was all cured(L+S138).[1]

Margaret's preoccupation with words and learning is illustrated through a rather curious mechanism that induces a major vision. Speaking of herself in the third person, she describes how she was puzzled, almost obsessed, by the meaning of a certain word:

> Not long ago some good people were together in a house and spoke of God. There was a worthy man who said that once he had asked a lady what the word "vehement" meant and that the lady had answered that it meant "strong." There was a person present who was deeply touched by this word, and it seemed to her that all this was of great importance, but she never dared to ask him to explain the word "vehement" to her.... This word was so deeply driven into her heart that she could not get rid of it (L+S143-144).

Margaret begins to pray and she is then transported into an open space where she finds an inverted dried up tree which is *inscribed* with words designating the five senses (L+S145). Then a great stream rushes down from a mountain and reverses the tree so that its branches which have begun to green now point towards heaven (L+S146).[2]

This vision represents a flowering and consequently a validation of the five corporeal senses. In her writings Margaret had several times referred to the different senses (both literally and metaphorically) and to their importance in experiencing God. In the *Page of Meditations*, for example, she had spoken of God as

---

1 The idea of the text as cure also appears in the thirteenth-century *chantefable Aucassin and Nicolette*. In the prologue we read:"nus homs.../.../ s'il l'oit, ne soit garis" (Everyone who hears it [the *chantefable*] will immediately be cured. Ll.10-14, ed. M. Roques, Paris: Champion, 1925). The theme of the"healing text" appears several times throughout the work.

2 See Roland Maissoneuve,"L'Expérience mystique et visionnaire de Marguérite d'Oingt," pp. 94-95 where he traces the idea of the tree in the scriptures (from the tree of Genesis to the tree of the kingdom of God in Matthew 13:31). He also points out that the inverted tree appears in other cultures. See his note 12 for the history of the idea of the five senses (going from Origen and Gregory of Nyssa via Saint Augustine to Saint Bernard of Clairvaux and Saint Bonaventure). He also examines the role the five senses play in the visions of other female mystics. Gertrud of Helfta, for example, writes of"the beatitudes of the five senses." In the *Herald of Divine Love* she describes Christ's union with the soul effected through the five senses.

"the glorious rose in which are all good odors and colors" (P25), and in the *Mirror* God

> is the sweet electuary in which are all good flavors. He is so good that all who taste Him will be all the more hungry the more they receive and they will not dare to desire anything but the sweetness they feel from Him. (M31)

What is important in the vision of the tree is that the *words* for the five senses are inscribed on the tree. The experiences which could be transmitted directly through the senses thus seem to be mediated by writing. Consequently, in order to understand the meaning of the tree—and to experience God—one has to be able to read. The interpretation of the vision is thus built-in, as it were, and it is bound up with reading and writing.

The divine activation of the senses evident in the reversal and the greening of the tree also extends to Margaret's activities: her earthly transcription of God's holiest revelations is a legitimate enterprise. She is God's legitimate scribe, she is the one who finally speaks of the "unspeakable" with God's permission and support.

* * *

The theme of writing winds its way through all of Margaret's works. For her, as for many female mystical writers, is was initially a source of conflict. But God's grace enabled her to overcome her reluctance to write and to turn her visions into a source of authority. By stressing the curative powers of writing, its permanence, its usefulness as a basis for meditations, Margaret fully appropriated a part of her culture that was becoming more and more literate. She showed that women participated fully in this writing culture and that they did so by divine sanction and command.

Index